THE MAN

on the

ASSEMBLY LINE

By Charles R. Walker
and Robert H. Guest

INSTITUTE OF HUMAN RELATIONS
YALE UNIVERSITY

Published by HARVARD UNIVERSITY PRESS

CAMBRIDGE · MASSACHUSETTS · 1952

ACKNOWLEDGMENTS

Unfortunately, it is impossible to acknowledge individually our indebtedness to the many contributors to this book. We are especially grateful for the courtesy and the coöperation of members of management, of union officials, and of the workers of the plant studied.

Grateful acknowledgment is made to Daniel Colyer, Sig Nosow, and Stuart L. Knowlton, who, as graduate students of the Department of Industrial Relations of the Massachusetts Institute of Technology, conducted the bulk of the interviews with workers in the summer of 1949. The authors are grateful to Mrs. Joyce E. H. Randall for technical assistance, and to Mrs. Frank Logue for the final editing of the manuscript.

The book owes much to the valuable suggestions of Mark A. May, Director of the Institute of Human Relations, to Wendell Bennett, Chairman of the Department of Anthropology, and to E. Wight Bakke, Director of the Labor and Management Center, of Yale University.

ACKNOWLEDGMENTS

CONTENTS

TABLES

CHARTS

LIST OF ILLUSTRATIONS

FOREWORD

The research reported in this monograph is on the satisfactions that workers on an automobile assembly line derive from their jobs. A representative sample of 180 workers was interviewed in their homes with a schedule designed to bring out facts, attitudes, and opinions about their jobs, their relations to fellow workers and supervisors, working conditions, pay and promotions, and relations to the union. The results throw new light on the controversial question of the influence of paced and repetitive work on the satisfactions that men derive from their labors.

This is a pilot study. It prepares the way for more extensive investigations of workers on assembly lines. The authors are careful not to generalize the conclusions from their results beyond the particular plant studied. Similar studies in a representative number of plants are needed before general conclusions can be reached. The authors expect to proceed with further studies as soon as possible.

Aside from the practical suggestions concerning changes in the management of assembly lines that may accrue from this and similar studies, the assembly line itself may prove to be a valuable laboratory for the study of many important aspects of human behavior. Nowhere else can be found thousands of people doing the same things over and over for several hours a day and, in many instances, for the whole productive lifetime of the worker. A number of basic social and psychological problems are suggested by the present study. For example, the authors found in this plant a few workers who reported that they were quite happy doing simple repetitive and paced jobs. What are the personality characteristics of such persons? The authors also found that a job requiring either a minimum or a maximum amount of attention is more satisfying than one that demands a degree of attention in between these two extremes. This suggests another interesting psychological problem.

The authors make it clear that this study was done in the public interest. Its main purpose was to increase the general store of knowledge concerning the adjustments of workers to their physical and social environments and to the characteristics of their jobs. The Institute of Human Relations is grateful to the management, the workers, and the union at this particular plant for their generous coöperation.

Mark A. May, *Director*
Institute of Human Relations
Yale University

January 2, 1952

THE MAN
ON THE ASSEMBLY LINE

THE MAN ON THE ASSEMBLY LINE

INTRODUCTION

*Machines alone do not give us mass production. Mass
production is achieved by both machines AND men.
And while we have gone a long way toward perfect-
ing our mechanical operations, we have not successfully written into our equations whatever complex
factors represent Man, the human element.*
— Henry Ford II.

In less than thirty years mass production has transformed the industrial base of the United States. Over
the next fifty — or less — it seems not unreasonable to
predict that it may transform the world's economy. New methods
are constantly being discovered, and new sectors of industry
captured by them. Nevertheless, what has already taken place
has a certain unity. As early as 1926, a government report began:
"There is taking place in the United States today a new industrial
revolution which may far exceed in economic importance that
older industrial revolution . . . which occurred in England in the
last quarter of the eighteenth century, and which eventually
transformed English industrial, political and social life . . . We
are at the present time experiencing what is perhaps the most

remarkable advance in productive efficiency in the history of the modern industrial system." *

It is now widely accepted that mainly out of this "revolution" came the advance in material well-being in the United States between the two world wars. Between 1919 and 1939, mass production methods matured and by the end of that period had captured the dominant sectors of the American economy. In American manufacturing, productivity per man per working hour doubled; in automobiles, an advanced sector, productivity tripled.

But besides creating a higher standard of living — and a different one — machines and the methods of organizing men around them have created a new *environment* for modern man. It is a part of this environment, the environment of modern man at work, which this volume is designed to explore. The machine will be surveyed less as a tool for production than as a part of the topography of a man's work place, and mass production not as an engineering method but as a code of law governing his behavior and way of life in the factory.

Professor William F. Ogburn, of the University of Chicago, has vividly expressed a similar idea: "There is reason to remark that the inventors of the automobile have had more influence than Caesar, Napoleon and Ghengis Khan. . . The environment of modern man is made up of machines much as the environment of wild animals is made up of fauna, flora, wind, rain and temperature." **

What are some of the problems which an "environment of machines" in a mass production work place pose for men and management and for the society of which they are both members?

An elementary problem area is certainly the one of "adjustment" from the old to the new surroundings. Individuals react

* Ewan Clague, "Index of Productivity of Labor in the Steel, Automobile, Shoe, and Paper Industries," *Monthly Labor Review*, July, 1926, vol. XXIII, no. 1, p. 1.

** William Fielding Ogburn, *Technological Trends and National Policy, Report of the Sub-committee on Technology to the U. S. National Resources Committee* (Washington, D. C., 1947), pp. 4 and 8.

very differently to assembly lines. What, then, are the personality characteristics of those who adjust quickly to — and appear to thrive on — mechanically paced and repetitive jobs? What, on the other hand, are the personality characteristics of those who suffer mentally and physically on such jobs, and who perform them badly? Can the adjustment problem, in other words, be solved by selection? Or is the modern work environment simply *wrong* for the normal human being?

Or, to take an engineering and management approach: In the present state of the mechanical arts, what part of a worker's skill and power can the engineer build into a machine? What must he leave out? Precisely and to what extent in the most mechanized sectors of our economy does the human equation still affect quantity and quality?

Taking another approach, one may ask: If a man spends at least a third of his life in direct contact with a mass production environment, why shouldn't we consider as important (to him and to society) the hours of living time he spends inside the factory — as important and valuable, for example, as the product he produces which is consumed outside the factory? We talk of a high standard of living, but frequently mean a high standard of consumption. Man consumes in his leisure, but fulfills himself not only in his leisure but in his work. Is our mass production work environment making such fulfillment impossible?

A short way to sum up these and a great many more questions is: To what degree can — or should — men be "adjusted" to the new environment of machines, and to what degree is it possible to adjust or rebuild that environment to fit the needs and personalities of men?

Research for *The Man on the Assembly Line* was begun in the summer of 1949 on one of the most modern automobile assembly lines in the world. In order to preserve more easily the anonymity of those who freely supplied information, managers, workers, and union leaders, the plant has been called Plant X. One hundred and eighty workers were interviewed in their homes over a period of months concerning all phases of their life on "the line." These workers constituted a substantial and stratified sample of the total number of productive workers in the plant.

Nearly 90 per cent of the men working at Plant X came from jobs where the pace of work was not machine-governed in a strict sense and from jobs over 72 per cent of which were not repetitive. In short, the area from which they were recruited had few mass production factories. One might say, then, that these men were representative of the majority of workers who in the past thirty years have made the transition from occupations characteristic of the first industrial revolution to work environments characteristic of the second.

The comparatively recent character of the several scientific and technological revolutions through which we have passed perhaps helps to explain why the new geography of man-at-work has received so little scientific study. The new science, or art, of human relations in industry is, to be sure, continually throwing light on the field, but expeditions specifically organized to explore the area have been rare.

There have been collateral studies. An important literature bearing on man's relation to his work has grown up, for example, through the study of fatigue. Notable here is the early work of the Medical Research Council in England and the later work of the Harvard Fatigue Laboratory. In England, as a follow-up of its earlier studies which were largely concerned with physiological fatigue, there came the pioneering work of Wyatt and Frazer on monotonous and repetitive jobs, on what the authors called "mental fatigue." Earlier research into the psychological effects of machine work had been undertaken by the Swiss psychologist, Leon Walther, at Geneva.

Most discussed, but perhaps least studied in a systematic fashion, have been the work environments of assembly lines, and particularly of assembly lines in the automobile industry.* Yet it would appear to be this sector which exemplifies in its most advanced form the problems of man and the machine. Here the authors believe the characteristics of a mass production job may be more easily isolated and studied in their impact on the individual. Here also the effects of the mass production method in altering the structure of in-plant society may be sharply delineated.

This book is intended for the professional student of industrial society, but it is hoped that other persons, in business, labor, and the professions, may find it of interest and value. The exploration proceeds slowly, especially in the middle chapters. These the general reader may wish to skip through rapidly. The authors have felt it necessary, because of the newness of the territory, to take frequent compass readings.

The man on the assembly line at Plant X was full of ideas for altering the topography of his own work surroundings in the interest both of greater personal satisfaction and of greater productive efficiency. These ideas and some of their implications have been embodied in the concluding section of this book. Some of these suggestions we believe may be generally adopted in comparable situations. To be successful it is our belief that they should be carried out with the coöperation of both union and management. To the authors the suggestions made by the workers have been of use in formulating questions more sharply for future research and experiment.

Aside from practical recommendations, it is hoped that this study may point the way to deeper and wider explorations of the work environment of modern man in the interest of behavioral theory. As Professor Mark May suggests, "The assembly line itself

* A critical discussion and survey of existing literature on assembly lines in general and their bearing on human behavior may be found in Chapter II, "Esquisse d'une Psycho-sociologie du Travail a la Chaine," of Professor Georges Friedmann's *Ou va le Travail humain?* (Gallimard, 1950).

may prove to be a valuable laboratory for the study of many important aspects of human behavior."

The Machine and its impact on Man has long been a favorite theme of philosophers, social historians, and propagandists. In the field of propaganda — and also of pure speculation — the intellectual and the businessman have frequently been on opposite sides of the argument. Here "intellectual" signifies the man who thinks about machines inside a factory without having any personal or professional experience with them. Among such are many ideological "machine wreckers." They would like to see most machines abolished and the technological geography of the twentieth century revert to the simplicity of the fifteenth. Finally, they deplore the machine as a robot maker and a destroyer of soul and body.

In contrast is the man who holds that all technological innovations are beneficent and a blessing for all. This was the characteristic mood of the last century. Now, in the second half of the twentieth, most thoughtful persons are aware of some of the problems, as well as the bright promises and substantial benefits, of a technological civilization. To believe that the nineteenth-century optimist was "wrong" and the twentieth-century pessimist or skeptic "right" is to miss the point. There are tasks appropriate not only to days of the week but also to centuries. A major task, it may be argued, of the nineteenth century and part of the twentieth was to rough out the technological topography of the modern world. The task of the second half — if we preserve it from destruction — is to make it a good place in which to live.

"But the Machine is not an end," writes Saint-Exupéry, author of *Man and the Earth*. "It is a tool . . . like the plow. If we believe that it degrades Man, it is possibly because we lack the perspective for judging the end results of transformations as rapid as those to which we have been subjected. What are the hundred years in the history of the Machine when compared with two hundred thousand years in the history of Man? We have scarcely established ourselves in this country of mines and of central electricity. It is as if we had hardly begun to live in the new house that we have not yet finished building. Everything has changed so rapidly around us: human relations, conditions of work, customs. . . Every step in our progress has driven us a little further from our acquired habits, and we are in truth pioneers who have not yet established the foundations of our new country." *

* From *Terre des Hommes*, Antoine de Saint-Exupéry (Paris: Gallimard, 1939), p. 58.

1 THE PROBLEM STATED

Of all occupations in modern industry none has attracted such controversial comment as that of the assembly worker, and especially of the auto assembly worker on the "final line." The extraordinary ingenuity that has gone into the construction of automobile assembly lines, their perfected synchronization, the "all but human" or "more than human" character of the machines, the miracle of a car rolling off the conveyor each minute under its own power — all this has caught and held the world's imagination for a quarter of a century. On the other hand, extreme subdivision of labor (the man who puts a nut on a bolt is the symbol) conjoined with an "endlessly moving belt" has made the assembly line the classic symbol of the subjection of man to the machine in our industrial age. Perhaps it is because neither the observers who have been attracted nor those who have been repelled by this dramatic picture have been willing to risk any disturbance of their emotions that so little scientific study has been devoted to human relations on an assembly line.

A first requirement for our inquiry is to define the characteristics of auto assembly work. To begin with, however, auto assembly work is merely one case, although an important and dramatic one, of the application of mass production methods to modern industry. The prior requirement, then, is to define the *general* characteristics of the mass production method.

Although the methods of mass production or, more accurately and specifically for our purposes, the methods of *progressive manufacture*, have been defined and discussed in different ways by different writers it is agreed by nearly everyone that these methods derive from at least two fundamental and related ideas, *standardization* and *interchangeability*. By accurately standardizing the constituent parts of a gun, Eli Whitney showed that any one part of any one gun could be substituted for the corresponding part of any other gun. In other words, they were interchangeable, just as today one crank shaft of an automobile of a given make and model can be substituted for any other crank shaft of the same make and model. Given these basic ideas plus the accurate machining methods which made them applicable to manufacture, Ford was able to work out and apply the three following additional "principles" of progressive manufacture:

(1) The orderly progression of the product through the shop in a series of planned operations arranged so that the right part always arrives at the right place at the right time.

(2) The mechanical delivery of these parts and of the product as it is assembled to and from the operators.

(3) A breakdown of operations into their simple constituent motions.*

Let us now look at these familiar principles or techniques as they are translated into the work experience of individual men and women in mass production factories. A man's work is brought to him, together with needed parts or tools, rather than the man going to his work. This bringing is done, as a rule, by mechanical means — a conveyor, belt, or trolley, for example. When a given piece of work is finished, it is carried forward, also by mechanical

* This is a rephrased and slightly more explicit statement of the three principles of mass production as set down in the article on "Mass Production" by Henry Ford in the *Encyclopedia Britannica*, XV, 14th ed. Ford's phrasing of the three principles is as follows:

"1. The planned orderly progression of the commodity through the shop.
"2. The delivery of work instead of leaving it to the workmen's initiative to find it.
"3. An analysis of operations into their constituent parts."

means, to the next worker. From the standpoint of the individual worker, therefore, the important fact is that the *pace* of his work is being controlled mechanically, rather than by such means as a written schedule or the verbal direction of his foreman.

There is great variation in the type of transportation within the factory for material, work, or parts. There is also great variation in the speed of transportation, in the weight of parts and tools, and, finally, in the length of the work cycles assigned to individuals. None of these variations, however, affects the central principle, movement of work units and parts to and from the worker, which results in a mechanical pacing of the worker.

Mass production jobs differ widely as to the degree of physical energy required. Whether little or much, however, almost all demand that the worker's energy be expended at regular and precisely defined intervals. Particularly on a conveyor mechanically paced, this means that there is no opportunity for a spurt and a lull in the expenditure of physical effort. Another way to say the same thing is that the worker cannot apply his own work rhythm but must adapt to the rhythm of the machine.

Since all "work" has been broken down into a series of simplified motions, with only a limited number assigned to any one individual, it follows that doing the same thing over and over is a natural characteristic of the mass production job. However, we shall find it important to emphasize that the degree of repetitiveness varies greatly from industry to industry and also from job to job within an industry.

Several other characteristics flow from the assignment of only a few operations to any one worker. One of these is that most jobs require a minimum of skill, so that the worker can learn to do his job adequately in a few days or a few weeks. Another characteristic which helps to explain why little skill is demanded: the worker has no choice in the selection of tools or methods on the job. They are predetermined for him through being a part of the fixed equipment of the factory. From these job characteristics it follows logically that in most mass production plants the worker has little contact with the whole product which the plant manufactures. In fact, he may never see it. Usually he works on only one part of that product, and often on a very small fraction of the one part.

Another characteristic relates to the quality of attention required of the worker. In any industrial field this will vary from jobs which demand intense and continuous mental attention to those which can be done automatically or "without thinking." Whatever the *degree* of attention required, there appears to be an important difference in the *quality* demanded by the average mass production job in comparison with other occupations. The difference may be roughly defined by the phrase *surface mental attention* as against mental attention in depth.

If the above description is correct, the characteristics of the average mass production job may be summarized as follows:

(1) Mechanical pacing of work.
(2) Repetitiveness.
(3) Minimum skill requirement.
(4) Predetermination in the use of tools and techniques.
(5) Minute subdivision of product worked on.
(6) Surface mental attention.

For the engineer all of the above characteristics are brought into focus in what is known as the *job cycle*. Each worker must perform a prescribed number of operations within a set time limit and, in the case of those working on moving conveyors, within a given distance along the line. This critical relation of time, motion, and distance is important to our present inquiry. Some workers perform a single operation in a short period of time, less than one minute, and in one location. At the other extreme, workers may perform as many as fifteen operations requiring as many as eight minutes and a hundred feet in distance as the product moves with the conveyor. The average job cycle at Plant X comprises one or two operations performed in two minutes' time.

When Plant X first went into production, the average cycle was longer both in time and number of operations. As the workers learned to perform their work more quickly and accurately, the speed of the conveyor was increased, more operators were added, and the length of the job cycle reduced. The average worker then performed fewer operations on the product in far less time, and the distance over which each worker traveled with the conveyor was shortened.

As remarked earlier, the auto assembler's job is considered as a specific case within the broader classification of mass production jobs. Does the "species" show important differences or refinements within the "genus?" Yes. Certain of the characteristics which have just been described in very general terms appear with a unique emphasis when applied to the auto assembler's job. This is especially true of points 1 and 6 mentioned above, mechanical pacing and surface mental attention.

Although nearly every industry has come to use mechanical conveyor systems, their earliest and still possibly most elaborate and complete utilization for the manufacture of a major product is in the automobile industry, and especially in "final assembly." The remark made by Mr. Ford in 1922 is still applicable: "Every piece of work in the whole shop moves. It may move on hooks, on overhead chains going to assembly in the exact order in which the parts are required; it may travel on a moving platform or it may go by gravity, but the point is that there is no lifting or trucking of anything except raw material." * We might add that today much of the raw material is also carried by a mechanical conveyor.

As to point 6, our observations suggest that the average auto assembler's job requires a relatively high and continuous degree of mental attention, a fact which has an important bearing on job satisfaction. There are many jobs in modern industry, including jobs on moving belts, which the worker can perform auto-

* Quoted by Charles Merz in *And Then Came Ford* (New York: Doubleday-Doran, 1929), pp. 198–220.

matically or "without thinking." On such jobs he may turn inward to his own thoughts or carry on connected conversations with his fellow workers. Such jobs are less fatiguing than those which, though without special skill, require a high and continuous degree of mental attention without accompanying mental absorption.* Our own observation is that a majority of automobile assembly jobs fall, with variations as to degree, into the latter category.

A word should be said regarding the amount of physical energy demanded of the automobile assembly worker as compared with workers in other industries. If jobs be classified as heavy, moderate, or light, a majority of auto assembly jobs may be described as moderate to heavy. This is an important fact. The degree of physical effort required on jobs that are mechanically paced and repetitive often makes the difference between satisfaction and dissatisfaction. For example, many jobs in American industry have all the mass production characteristics we have listed but are "light" as regards physical effort. This fact makes them acceptable to many persons who could not make a satisfactory adjustment to auto assembly work.

The six characteristics which we have defined above, then, we shall apply to the assembly line in Plant X, noticing any differences or exceptions. To do this will be, of course, merely a requisite and elementary step toward the main object of this inquiry: to explore the relation between the work environment of an auto assembly line and the assembly man's satisfaction or dissatisfaction on the job.

It is evident that the several characteristics of assembly line work which have been defined and listed above apply only, or chiefly, to the worker's experience with the *immediate content* of his job. This is an important point. Consider a typical job on

---

* This point was noted by the investigators for the British Industrial Fatigue Research Board. See Report no. 56 (1929), *The Effects of Monotony in Work,* S. Wyatt and J. A. Fraser, assisted by F. B. L. Stock, pp. 42, 43; also, Report no. 82 (1938), *The Machine and the Worker: A Study of Machine-feeding Processes,* S. Wyatt and J. N. Langdon, assisted by F. B. L. Stock.

the assembly line at Plant X which consists in taking the visor off a moving trolley and installing it as the car moves slowly down the line. It takes the worker slightly over a minute to do the installation. Clearly the visor installer experiences here, in his immediate job, the factors of a conveyor-paced task, of a repetitive one, of one that concerns only a minute fraction of the final product, and so forth. These mass production characteristics, then, apply to the content of the worker's immediate job experience, but they do not apply to, nor have they told anything about, many other important job characteristics. For example, they do not tell how much pay the worker gets for installing visors, how good or how bad his relations are to his foreman, whether the factory is clean and well lighted, how fast he will be promoted from visor-installer to another position, how steady Plant X employment is, or whether the worker belongs to an active union, and so forth.

Any study of job satisfaction in any plant which omitted such factors would obviously be of little value. A few years ago, American employers were apt to say that "the only thing the worker cares about is what goes into his pay envelope." Today it is hardly necessary to dispute the inaccuracy of such a statement, or to point to the prejudices behind it. Today the multiple nature of job satisfaction or dissatisfaction — a principle which has always recommended itself to the common sense of factory managers — has now been documented by a very large number of scientific studies on employee attitudes.

What, then, are the major elements which should be included in a picture of the *total job situation* at Plant X as elements of satisfaction or dissatisfaction? Below is the classification we have adopted:

(1) The worker's immediate job.
(2) His relations to fellow workers.
(3) Pay and security.
(4) His relation to supervision.

(5) General working conditions in the plant.

(6) Promotion and transfer.

(7) His relation to the union.

In each chapter, we treat one of these elements in its own right, so to speak, and then seek its evaluation with reference to all the other elements in the total job situation. Our aim has been to put each element into perspective, but particularly the element of "immediate job content" on which mass production methods so directly impinge. To summarize our reasoning: mass production jobs have certain characteristics. Auto assembly work shares those characteristics. Most of these impinge directly on the immediate content of the auto assembler's job. That content may give him satisfaction or dissatisfaction, or he may be indifferent to it. To know whether it gives him one or the other, or neither, is important. But it is also important to know *how the worker himself rates immediate job content within the total picture of job elements.*

In addition to these relationship categories, it was our original intention to explore the satisfactory or unsatisfactory character of relations to staff and service personnel, such as maintenance men and inspectors. Our exploratory interviews, however, turned up so little significant material in this area that we dropped the category.

The above classification of elements recommended itself for a number of reasons. Judging by previous studies in job satisfaction and by our preliminary interviews, the categories included the principal elements given by workers as reasons for liking or disliking their jobs. Although it would obviously be unsuited to a study of middle or top management in a mass production plant, this classification seemed well adapted to a manual-worker-centered study.

For each of these several major elements in the total job picture at Plant X we have followed a simple pattern of presentation: (1) the facts of the element; (2) attitudes of the workers toward these facts; (3) evaluation of the importance of the particular job element within the total job picture.

To illustrate, when the "workers' relations with supervision" are discussed, as they are in Chapter VII, a factual description of the supervisory structure is given first, together with a record of worker interaction with its different levels. Second, we record what they thought and felt about their supervisors. Finally, the workers' rating of this particular job element, *relations to supervision,* in the total job situation at Plant X is recorded. That rating should answer such questions as: Is a good boss more or less important to a worker than good pay or an interesting job (immediate job content), or good working conditions, or company benefits, or some other factor?

Mass production characteristics have both direct and indirect effects on job satisfaction. Machine pacing, repetitiveness, and the other characteristics bear on the worker directly through his immediate job, but they also have indirect effects operating through the social structure of the factory.

Here we may illustrate through one important part of the social structure of any factory, its system of promotion. By an extreme subdivision of the process into constituent motions, jobs are so fractionalized that no one job pays very much more than another. Hence the *ladder of promotion* regarding both skill and compensation is very greatly shortened. It calls for no great amount of imagination to assess the social and organizational consequences of this "effect."

A modern auto assembly line emphasizes a work environment with which millions of workers and thousands of managers are familiar. In that sense, the scope of reference of this study is very wide; in a stricter sense, however, our scope of reference is much narrower. To begin with, this is a study of a single mass production plant in a single industry. Further, Plant X was new, having been in operation only two years at the time of this study. Its workers were recruited mainly from an area which was unfamiliar with strict mass production methods; only two in our sample had ever worked in an automobile plant before. From these circumstances, it would seem reasonable to assume that, among other things, they would need a longer period of adjustment to assembly work than would workers from an area such as Detroit, where a whole population has been conditioned to a mass production outlook for many years.

Most Plant X workers came from jobs which paid them lower wages and offered them less job security than did their new assembly plant jobs. The age level was somewhat lower, the educational level somewhat higher than for the average automobile assembly worker.

Every plant in every industry will, of course, present variations in these and other characteristics. In future surveys of plants in different parts of the United States, the authors hope to determine the significance of these variations for the applicability of their findings.

At the same time, however, Plant X offered the investigators a unique scientific advantage anticipated in its selection for this pilot study. That was the use of the previous work experience for each man interviewed as a "control" in the analysis and evaluation of the characteristics of his new job at Plant X. Also, just because it was new, and just because it recruited workers from a small business area of fluctuating prosperity, the contrast between the new and the old work environments was sharp, not only objectively but in the minds of the men themselves.

This point is worth a brief elaboration. In preliminary — and partially undirected — interviews, we were struck by the repeated references to "my old job" and to comparisons between "my old" and "my new" job. Some workers contented themselves with very general comments when making comparisons. A majority moved into a point-by-point discussion of both jobs. They compared pay, type of work performed, skills demanded, working conditions, work companions, foremen, company policies, hours, and many other factors. For most of the workers interviewed, this recall was not difficult. Some had left previous jobs only eight months before. None had worked on his present job over two years. Nearly every man interviewed was thus able to make a vivid and specific comparison between two well-remembered work experiences.

The intention of this study, as suggested in the Introduction, is to explore the topography of a typical mass production environment. Another approach might have been to emphasize personality differences among workers and to seek correlations which possibly exist between them and adjustment to assembly line work. What, for example, were the personality characteristics of those who liked and those who disliked conveyor paced jobs? It is hoped in future research to seek answers to this type of question.

SUMMARY

(1) We are exploring the relation of auto assembly line work to satisfaction on the job.

(2) Auto assembly jobs are one "species" of mass production occupations.

(3) From the standpoint of the worker, mass production jobs have the following characteristics:

      (a) Mechanically controlled work pace.
      (b) Repetitiveness.
      (c) Minimum skill.
      (d) Predetermination of tools and techniques.
      (e) Minute subdivision of product.
      (f) Surface mental attention.

(4) More than many other mass production jobs, auto assembly jobs are characterized by an elaborate conveyor system, by a high mental attention requirement, and by relatively high expenditure of physical energy.

(5) Most of the six characteristics discussed above affect directly the immediate or intrinsic job of the worker. On this our interest in this study is centered.

(6) But we also study the whole job situation at Plant X in terms of its chief elements — pay, the promotion system, working conditions, the union, and so forth — in order to put "immediate job content" in an adequate perspective.

(7) In doing so, we give the worker's evaluation of the importance of each of these elements in the total situation. Each element is evaluated especially with reference to the worker's immediate job, to which auto assembly characteristics more directly apply.

(8) The technological factors of auto assembly work affect the worker, both directly and indirectly. They affect him directly through the immediate job, and indirectly by modifying the basic organizational and social structure of the plant. We also examine some aspects of this indirect influence.

(9) The scope of reference of this study is wide, in that it deals in general with a kind of work environment with which millions of workers and managers are familiar. More strictly, the reference of the study is limited: to a single new plant in a relatively low wage area where the workers have had little experience with the Plant X type of mass production job.

To conclude: In this inquiry into the nature of job satisfaction we seek to discover general principles and record the effects of mass production methods. It cannot be too strongly emphasized that such effects, whether desirable or undesirable, cannot be credited to any one industry, company, or plant. The effects and influences of such work environments as the one here described are characteristic phenomena of the industrial civilization under which we all of us live and most of us work. All the evidence suggests — and this, too, it is important to emphasize — that there is nothing immutable about the mechanisms which produce such effects, whether they be desirable or undesirable for human living. An objective record, it is hoped, will enable men to avoid the undesirable and relate more closely the desirable effects with technological requirements.

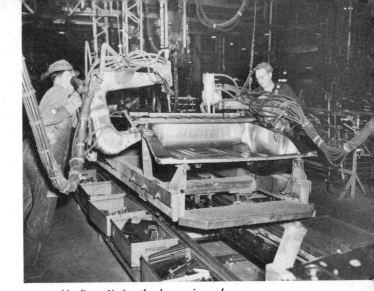

OT WELDING
etal Department

st operation on the main assembly line. Notice the large piece of
essed sheet steel fixed to the conveyor truck. This is the floor section of
e trunk compartment. Operators are welding other sections of the
derbody to it.

OWL ASSEMBLY
etal Department

ese two men are working together on welding jigs in subassembly of
wlings. Assembled cowlings are mounted on underbody shown mov-
g along on main line conveyor. They form main forward upright
pport of body.

Two-man team shown lowering body top and rear quarter panel secti onto undersection of the car body.

As conveyor carries car body along main line, operator grinds rou welded seams with air-powered grinder.

OOD FINISH
etal Department

ows hood grinding in sub-assembly area. Operators perform their
ork while riding on the conveyor or walking beside it. Storage area
hoods is at right.

NAMEL FINISH
int Department

dies move through paint spray booth as men spray enamel on the
dy top from paint guns. Notice paint hose lines on shed wall. Each
e carries a different color.

INSTRUMENT PANE
Trim Department

The two workers shown inside the car body are attaching pre-assembl instrument panel to dashboard. Worker at the left is putting on outsi trim.

INSIDE TRIM
Trim Departme

Shows part of main line conveyor system. Outside trim operations a complete; some inside trim work remains to be done. Few workers a visible, since most operations, inside molding and cloth trim, are pe formed inside the cars.

POLISHING
Paint Department

Workers polish body surfaces with power-driven rotary polishing wheels. Bodies at right are in "body bank" following trim operations. From far end of bank, bodies are trucked across to the polishers on the moving conveyor shown at left.

SEAT CUSHION INSTALLATION
Trim Department

Not all operations in an assembly plant are mechanized. Here two workers are shown moving, by hand, finished front seat into car body on the main line.

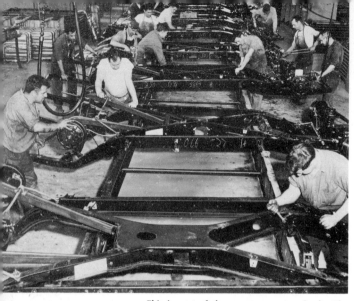

This is part of the conveyor system in the Chassis Department. Operato
are shown making adjustments on axle assemblies, springs, and brak
drums. Notice chassis frames are set crosswise and upside down on th
moving conveyor.

MOTOR MOUNT
Chassis Departme

As chassis frame moves, suspended from an overhead conveyor, worke
lower motor onto forward section of frame. Motor arrives on overhea
conveyors from stock. They have been assembled in another plant.

COMPLETED CHASSIS ASSEMBLY

Chassis Department

The chassis frame, complete with wheels, tires, steering column, motor, and so forth, is moving slowly into position for "body drop." Farther back, workers are making final adjustments on the frame.

BODY DROP

Final Line

Here completed body and completed chassis meet. The body which has been "dropped" — lowered through an opening in the floor above — is being guided into place. Notice the car still lacks front fenders, grille, hood, and so forth.

Here is a sub-assembly area close to the final line. Front fenders, grill
and radiators are assembled into single units by teams working on sta
tionary "bucks." Each completed unit is synchronized to travel by ove
head conveyor to its designated car on the final line.

FINAL LI

Assembly operations are now complete. Workers are shown making fir
adjustments and tests. Finished cars are driven off the line at an avera
rate of forty-five cars an hour.

2 PLANT OPERATIONS

In one sense Plant X is the final link in a series of highly synchronized operations which begin at the ore pits and coal mines and carry through into basic manufacturing and into the fabrication of "parts." At a prescribed moment in time and space these thousands of parts and units are brought to a focal point — the final assembly plant. Here the many products of previous operations are fed into a maze of conveyors and machinery and emerge as completed automobiles at the rate of over 350 each eight-hour day.

It is remarkable enough that all the products of previous operations from many different plants are processed, shipped, and arrive at the final assembly plant according to a precise schedule. But it is within the final operations that we find the most dramatic display of those factors so characteristic of mass production technology.

The production area of Plant X covers approximately a million square feet of ground floor space enclosed in a single building. Parallel rail spurs enter at two points some seven hundred feet apart. From one of these rail sidings materials are unloaded into a general area where car bodies are assembled; from the other siding parts are unloaded into another area where chassis assembly takes place.

Thus the entire plant is divided into two main areas with the operations of each beginning at a railroad siding. In one area the body is built up, painted and trimmed inside and out, and the upholstery installed. In the other area the motor, wheels, transmission, and so forth, are mounted on the chassis frame. The body and chassis are brought together and proceed down a final assembly line. Then they are tested, repaired, conditioned, and driven to an outside shipping yard.

The area given over to body operations, called the "body shop," is divided into three departments: Body in White (or Metal), Paint, and Trim. The other area, chassis assembly, is a single department known as Chassis. Each of these four production departments is headed by a superintendent, two to three general foremen, and nine to fifteen foremen. The staff and service departments, whose functions are not limited to any given production area, include Plant Engineering (Maintenance), Inspection, Personnel, Purchasing, Material and Production Control, Traffic, Car Distribution, Works Standards, and the Comptroller's Office.

Central to all production operations are two main assembly lines, one beginning in the Metal Department and the other in the Chassis Department. They converge later in the Chassis Department and continue as one line through the remaining final operations.

A simplified account of the work flow is given below. It is suggested that the reader follow the assembly of a car through each of the main operations shown in Figure 1.

We begin with the rail spur, RR[1], which enters the Metal Department (lower left on diagram). Here parts are unloaded and distributed to storage areas or directly to the line. Most of these parts are pre-formed metal sections which will be made up into sections of the automobile body. They include underbody pieces, cowlings, quarter panels, balloons (body tops), doors, and numerous other pieces. From storage these materials are moved into sub-assembly areas for metal processing and then onto the main line, or directly from a storage area to the line.

The main line itself starts at Point A in the Metal Department. A flat-surfaced dolly, known as a "body truck," is hitched to the conveyor chain and begins its course down the line. As it begins to move, the first piece of formed sheet metal, serving as the floor pan for the trunk compartment, is placed on the body truck. As the conveyor moves along, other under sections of the body

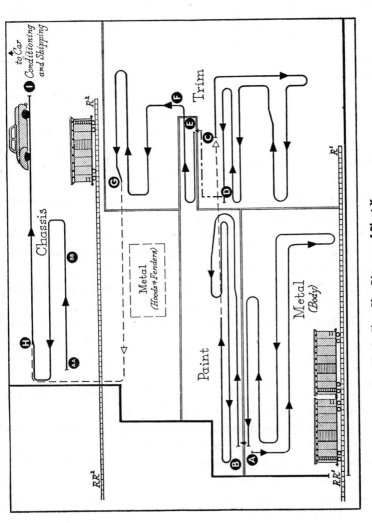

Fig. 1. Floor Plan Diagram of Plant X.

are placed on the truck and welded together. Gradually the general under-section of the body shell is assembled. Further on, cowlings, which have been made up in a sub-assembly area, are brought in and fixed to the underbody. Next, the rear quarter panels and the body tops are set in fixtures and welded to the panels and the underbody pieces. Now for several hundred feet the body truck moves through a series of spot and arc welding operations. Except for doors, the body shell may now be recognized as an actual car body. The remaining operations before painting are soldering, grinding, and the filing of welded seams. These are carried on throughout the remainder of the line in the area known generally as "Body Metal Finish." At a point midway along this line doors and trunk lids are conveyed from a storage area and attached to the body.

Close to its starting point, A, the conveyor ends and the body is transferred to a chain conveyor at B which carries another type of truck known as a "pallet." Here painting operations are begun, and for several hundred feet all operations fall within the jurisdiction of the Paint Department superintendent.

The first Paint Department operation is to clean the raw metal in preparation for a first coat of anti-rust, a process known as "bonderizing." The body is carried through an elongated metal shelter, then through a drying oven, and finally into a cooling booth. A prime coat of paint is sprayed on the body, after which the entire conveyor moves with the bodies to a second level of the building to pass through a series of drying ovens. When the conveyor returns the body to the main floor level, the prime surfaces are sanded. A preliminary coat of enamel is applied in a spray booth and "cooked" as the car passes through another oven. Similar operations are repeated three hundred feet down the line in a final paint booth.

With all painting complete, the body is ready to move into the Trim Department, where it receives most interior and exterior installations along a 2,000-foot line. These varied and complex operations include the installation of sound deadeners, door handles, body moldings, back windows, outside moldings, vent windows, interior trimmings (including all cloth trim), instrument panels, windshields, inside moldings, weather strippings, and many other material and accessory installations.

The trimmed body now comes to the second "break" in the main line at Point D. Here it is moved off the line and stored temporarily on body trucks in an area known as "body bank." At the proper scheduled time it is rolled off the storage or bank conveyor and again placed on the main conveyor at Point E.

Interestingly enough, in this area of operations the body returns briefly to the jurisdiction of the Paint Department. Here the body surfaces are polished. Midway along this line the rear fenders of certain types of bodies, which have passed through separate painting operations, are taken from an overhead conveyor and "hung" onto the body. They too are polished along with the rest of the outside surface. The hoods and front fenders are polished in this same general area and carried on conveyors to the final assembly area for installation. Polishing operations end when the conveyor moves into the area known as "body-fit-up," Point F, where seats and seat backs are installed and where other final body trimming is completed.

The body of the car is now complete. After a series of tests and repairs at the end of the trim line, the conveyor moves up an incline and onto a balcony at Point G, and for about five hundred feet no operations are performed. The finished body is simply in a state of storage-in-motion. It is lowered onto the proper chassis at the juncture of the Chassis and Body lines in a dramatic operation known as "body drop" at Point H.

While all these operations are taking place, another series has been started in the Chassis area of the plant. It began next to the other rail spur and was geared to the pace of the body operations so that at precisely the right moment a specified completed chassis meets a finished body at Body Drop.

The chassis operations begin where a "raw" chassis frame (main structural support of the automobile) is brought in from an outside storage area and placed on the main conveyor at Point AA. As it moves along the line, the spring and axle assemblies taken from rail cars at RR² are fixed to the chassis frame. After these and other assemblies are completed, the chassis is picked up by an overhead conveyor. The motor is mounted and secured on the frame at Point BB. Brake lines, under-body linkages, air cleaners, wheel and tire assemblies, and the steering column are attached in sequence.

After moving along approximately one thousand feet, the chassis is merged with the car body at Body Drop. On a signal from the ground floor to the second level, a body is picked up by a crane and lowered through an opening in the ceiling. Workers guide the body down and set it on the chassis. The car now moves eight hundred feet down the final line to the opposite end of the plant.

Several operations are performed on this final line, the principal ones being the installation of bumpers, front ends (grilles and front fenders), and hoods. Here final adjustments are also made, chiefly on the under parts of the car, in addition to many fittings, inspections, and tests.

Now the car, under its own propulsion, moves onto a set of rolls where the rear drive wheels are given a roll test. From this roll test the cars are sent to a separate car conditioning line where defects which were not caught previously are corrected. This car conditioning operation is really a little assembly line in itself.

Upon completion of conditioning operations, the car is washed and driven to the shipping area outside the plant in readiness for loading onto one of a fleet of trucks and delivery to a dealer.

Several of the operations described above are shown in the illustrations at the beginning of this chapter.

We have given a brief sketch of the physical layout of the plant, the work flow, and the principal departments, and illustrated certain typical operations. Actually, the technology is far more complicated than what we have delineated. The two main lines themselves are over two and a half miles long and move through literally hundreds of different operations in the assembly sequence. In addition to the main line conveyors, there are well over two miles of overhead conveyor lines which transport small parts, materials, and unit assemblies to appropriate places along the main line.

Hardly mentioned in the above description were the hundreds of sub-assembly operations located throughout the plant which feed into different sections along the line. One sub-assembly operation, seat cushion fabrication, is a complete assembly line in itself and occupies over fourteen thousand square feet of work space and equally as much again for storage. There are at least ten other major sub-assembly operations which occupy somewhat smaller areas. Each of these in turn has its own shorter sub-assembly lines and benches. In addition to the major sub-assembly operations, there are many small operations at benches and bucks immediately beside the main conveyor.

Further, Plant X does not produce one particular model of a given make of car. Rarely do any two identical models roll off the line in sequence. A blue coupe of one make may be followed by a green sedan of another make and further back on the line may be still another model of a third make of car. With over eighty models for all three makes together and over thirty different colors, it is remarkable that thirty to forty-five cars are sent off the line within the space of one hour.

A system such as this requires the utmost care in planning and scheduling. Even before the single piece of formed sheet metal is placed on the body truck in the Metal Department it is necessary to work out the complicated scheduling of other parts to be set in motion at the proper time intervals. Only in this way can the right part arrive at the right place at exactly the right time.

Of course, each individual part is not predetermined for any specific vehicle. Parts fabrication in other plants is so standardized that for any given model any front fender for that model may be drawn from stock and installed — parts are interchange-

able. Some parts such as simple bolts can be used in the fabrication of any make or model.

But the fact remains that once a door, grille, fender, motor, or
wheel has been set in motion on the conveyors, it must arrive at
the proper time and place in order to go on a designated model.
Any mistiming at any point may cause a delay in the total system
of operations along the main line. Scheduling information is
communicated chiefly by means of teletype machines located at
key check points throughout the plant. In a few seconds time one
section of the plant can notify other sections to expect schedule
changes on a particular order.

Even from this rapid tour of an assembly line, it is hoped that
some of the basic ideas underlying the methods of progressive
manufacture may have become vivid. The overwhelming impression is of movement. Two great conveyor lines move hundreds
of miles a day carrying the car body and the chassis, and feeding
in from overhead is a maze of smaller conveyors bringing parts
and assemblages to and from the worker.

This whole complex of operations demands the perfect synchronization of men and machines. For the engineer the complex
represents a physical application of three basic principles of mass
production — the orderly progression of the work through the
plant, the mechanical delivery of parts to and from the workers,
and finally the breakdown of operations into simple constituent
motions. For the worker these principles clearly define the role
he plays in the total picture. They determine the character of his
immediate job, the structure of his social relations, and, in short,
his total work environment.

3 FROM THE OLD JOB TO THE NEW

In many occupations in the modern world, the immediate content of a man's job is often of less importance to him than a half dozen other features of his employment. He may, for example, derive his greatest satisfaction — or dissatisfaction — from the people he works with, from the people he meets, from his immediate supervisor, from the prestige of his job, the money it pays or the benefits or perquisites that go with it, or, as is often true with young men, from the opportunity to learn enough to climb to a higher rung on the job ladder. The prominence of these factors in the minds of many social scientists perhaps explains why they have been investigated more thoroughly than the components and contents of a man's immediate job. Such an investigation is the subject of this chapter and the next.

Everyone agrees that there are some occupations where the content and immediate conditions of the work are of more than usual importance. Two extreme examples will make the point. The immediate content of an artist's job, creative use of paint and canvas, is presumably one very basic reason why the artist chose his particular occupation. The hazards of a deep-sea diver's job, the excitement, and certainly the physical conditions of his daily work are so prominent that it is hardly necessary to argue their "importance" to the worker.

As suggested earlier, it is partly because of what appeared to be the importance of his *immediate* job and its technological environment to the automotive assembly worker that we undertook this study. The reader is to be reminded that there is little objective or systematic evidence in this field. There is no body of reliable data, for example, on the comparative weight which the average worker in any given assembly plant gives to the different components of his immediate job. Nor is there evidence of the relative importance, for satisfaction or dissatisfaction, in the worker's mind of job content in comparison with pay, supervision, working conditions, or any other element in the total job situation of an auto assembly plant. In this chapter and the next we shall begin to present evidence on these points for the workers in Plant X. As mentioned in the Introduction, we are using previous job experience as a control in considering each element in the present job situation. Here such data may appropriately serve as an introduction to the immediate job content and to the technological environment of the assembly workers in Plant X.

The most significant fact about the previous job experiences of Plant X workers is that they bore little resemblance to the work of an automobile assembler. This was true for all but a handful of those recruited for Plant X. The bearing of this fact on our study was twofold: (1) It enabled most of the workers interviewed to describe clearly and vividly their present jobs by contrasting them with previous ones. (2) It probably increased the difficulties of adjustment to the new Plant X jobs.*

Table 1 gives a rough breakdown of occupational types on previous jobs, categorized under the system used in the *Dictionary of Occupational Titles*.** As might be expected, most of the men had done manual work, 75.5 per cent in all.† Notice, how-

---

* A limited amount of evidence is available upon this point. It is hoped that studies of workers on other automobile assembly lines will throw further light on problems of the early adjustment period.
** Government Printing Office.
    † Unless otherwise noted, the percentage figures given here and throughout the remainder of this study are based, in general, on the sample of 180, or 21 per cent of a restricted population of 848 production workers at Plant X. The method of sampling is reviewed on pp. 167 ff. of Appendix A, "Method of Research." On the basis of a 21 per cent sample, if simple random sampling from an unrestricted population were used, the conservative Standard Error (P = .50) would be approximately 3 per cent. More reliability than 3 per cent may be assumed since (a) the population was restricted and (b) the group was stratified according to seven basic factors of the work force.

ever, that 15 per cent of the men were drawn from the professional-managerial or clerical and sales group. The remainder came from service occupations, from agriculture and fishing, and a small number had had no previous job experience.

TABLE 1

Previous Job Experience of Production Workers at Plant X [a]
Based on Nine Occupational Groupings Listed in the
Dictionary of Occupational Titles

Code Digest	Type of Occupation	Number of Men
0	Professional or managerial	11
1	Clerical and sales	16
2	Service	8
3	Agriculture, fishing, and kindred occupations	5
4	Skilled in manufacturing and related activities	18
5	Skilled in nonmanufacturing and related activities	29
6	Semiskilled in manufacturing and related activities	45
7	Semiskilled in nonmanufacturing and related activities	31
8	Unskilled in manufacturing and related activities	—
9	Unskilled in nonmanufacturing and related activities	13
	No previous occupation	4
	Total	180

[a] Sample of 180 production workers.

Within the manual group, certain important distinctions should be made. Forty-seven men (Code Digits 4 and 5) had been skilled workers or foremen. In other words, 34.5 per cent of all those with manual work experience were skilled persons. Considering the relatively unskilled nature of automobile assembly work, this high proportion of skilled workmen among those recruited for Plant X is of interest.

The largest number (42.2 per cent) of men had held semiskilled jobs prior to working at Plant X. What kind of jobs had these been? The principal industries or businesses in which the men were engaged may be seen in Table 2. Notice that the variety and diversity in the types of industry and business is considerable, ranging from construction to communications, and from shoe manufacturing to shipbuilding. One industry is notable for its small representation: only two men had worked on an automobile assembly line before. Of the 176 persons who had held some kind of job previously, there had been eighty-three directly connected with manufacturing and ninety-three in a business not connected with manufacturing. In other words, slightly over half of the men in our sample had held jobs which were not directly related to manufacturing; they had not been in any activity which was in any respect similar to that at Plant X.

The figures in Table 2 are deceptive in one respect. It would appear that few workers were engaged in agriculture. This is not strictly true. Many of the men interviewed did considerable part-time work on farms or in their own large truck gardens. Even many who derived no income from farming lived in distinctly rural sections of small towns. We had been advised in advance to watch this factor closely. Although it is not documented as precisely as we would have desired, the characteristics of rural "independence" did appear to have some bearing on job attitudes at Plant X.

We are now ready to look at old jobs and new ones in terms of the mass production characteristics we have already discussed. To what degree were the previous jobs of Plant X workers controlled as to pace by a machine? How much skill did they demand? To answer these and other questions, every worker was asked to describe in detail both his old job and his new. These descriptions were then analyzed from the standpoint of the six basic characteristics. Table 3 gives the results with regard to the first characteristic, mechanically determined work pace.

The most obvious fact emphasized by Table 3 is that 154 (87.4 per cent) of the men now working at Plant X had come from jobs where pace was determined primarily by the individual worker.

TABLE **2**

Previous Employment of Production Workers at Plant X by Manufacturing and Nonmanufacturing Occupations [a]

Type of Occupation	Number of Men	
Manufacturing		
Shoes	20	
Textiles	12	
Machining	10	
Paper	7	
Plastics	6	
Iron and steel (fabricating)	6	
Electrical (household & industrial products)	5	
Batteries	4	
Clocks and watches	2	
Food processing	2	
Automobile assembly	2	
Aircraft	2	
Household products	2	
Rubber	1	
Hats	1	6
Subtotal		82
Nonmanufacturing		
Construction (building & highways)	20	
Auto repair	14	
Retail (groceries, household goods & services, eating establishments)	16	
Farming and horticulture	6	
Federal government	6	
Transportation (trucking and shipping)	5	
Repair and maintenance	5	
Routemen (food and beverage)	4	
Gasoline (retail)	3	
Municipal government	3	
Hospitals	3	
Shipbuilding	2	
Communications	1	
Entertainment	1	
Model-making	1	
State government	1	
Railroading	1	
Quarrying	1	
Subtotal		93
No previous employment	4	
Not known	1	
Subtotal		5
Total		180

[a] Sample of 180 production workers.

A large number in this group had been piece workers in small products manufacturing plants. Whether they maintained a high or low work pace was a matter, at least within limits, for the individual to decide. Another large group had held jobs in machine and auto repair shops where they had worked on "job assignments." Though in many cases there was a compulsion to com-

TABLE **3**

Work Pace Determinants on Previous Jobs

Determinant	Number of Men	Per Cent
Individual worker	154	87.4
Schedule	8	4.5
Machine	7	4.0
Other factors	7	4.0
Total	176[a]	99.9

[a] Percentages for previous job data are based on a total of 176: four workers indicated no previous employment.

plete a job as quickly as possible, the pace at which a man worked was at least to some degree his own problem, not determined by a machine or conveyor.

A wide range of jobs made up the remainder of the category of worker-determined pace. This included construction work, retail trades, service stations, custodial, landscaping, clerical, supervisory, and other kinds of work. The small group whose pace was determined by a schedule were men on milk routes, delivery truck drivers, and so forth.

Only seven (4 per cent) out of the entire sample had held jobs where pace was strictly machine governed. Most of these men had worked on moving belts or conveyors in battery plants, electrical assembly factories, and paper mills.

Since we are studying only the production workers in Plant X, for whom pace is determined by the moving conveyor, it is evident that most of the workers experienced a sharp change in this job factor when they went on their new jobs. They had come from job situations where pace was mainly determined by the man himself to a job situation where pace was mainly determined by the machine.*

Repetitiveness ** was the second job characteristic mentioned earlier as especially associated with mass production jobs and assembly line work. What about this characteristic as related to the previous jobs of the men interviewed? One hundred and twenty-one of the old jobs could properly be described as not repetitive; the remaining forty-seven were mostly or completely repetitive.† Thus, 72 per cent of the jobs the men held before they came to Plant X were not "repetitive" jobs. In contrast, only 14 per cent of the automobile assembly plant jobs could be considered as not being repetitive.

A third difference for a majority of the workers at Plant X between their old and new jobs was a drop in the amount of skill demanded. Applying learning time as a rough measure of skill, sixty-nine (39.2 per cent) of the workers stated that it took them less than a month to learn their old jobs; 107 (60.8 per cent) said it took them more than a month. On the new jobs these figures almost exactly reversed themselves: 118 (65.5 per cent) of the workers said it took them less than a month; sixty-one (33.9 per cent) said it took them more than a month.‡

Strikingly, our sample contains a considerable number of men who came into assembly line work at Plant X from jobs which had required very considerable experience or skill. Twenty-seven, for example, stated that the jobs from which they came had taken them from two to five years to learn; three from jobs which had taken them over five years to learn.

The fact that assembly line jobs require far less learning time than many, if not most, other jobs in modern industry is common

* There are, however, in Plant X, important differences between jobs in the degree of that determination. We shall look at these differences presently as well as at their effects on worker satisfaction.

** In this discussion we frequently use the term "variety" as the opposite or counterpart of "repetitiveness."

† Data incomplete on previous job descriptions of eight additional respondents (4.5 per cent).

‡ Learning time was indeterminate for one respondent.

knowledge. Our learning time tabulations, however, do something beyond registering this expected result. As we shall see, youth received a strong accent at Plant X. The average age for the sample interviewed was twenty-seven. Even for the majority of the younger men, taking a job in Plant X meant they were to exercise less skill than they had already acquired and had been used to applying on their previous jobs. The fact that the present job required less skill may have made it more or less desirable to the individual worker, depending upon a whole range of factors from pay to personality and education.

The educational level at Plant X was higher than that of other assembly plants within the same company: 81 per cent of the men had attended at least one year of high school, and 49 per cent were high-school graduates or more. We found evidence that some men felt their education had fitted them for jobs of higher skill than assembly work demanded.

Our learning time tabulations confirm the common knowledge that assembly line jobs take less time to learn than many other industrial jobs, but they also serve to discredit a popular illusion that *all* assembly jobs can be learned in a few days, if not a few hours. Forty-three of our sample said that it took them from one to six months to learn their jobs. These estimates by the individual workers correspond roughly with learning times allocated by supervision. The criterion used by supervision on whether a worker had learned his job was his ability to perform a prescribed number of operations without assistance and within a set time cycle.

Closely related to the factors of pace, repetitiveness, and skill is the question of job planning and the use of tools and materials. This factor, it is known from other studies, means much to some manual workers, little to others. A study of the characteristics of previous jobs held by Plant X assembly workers shows that 113 (62.7 per cent) were either partly or entirely free to determine how the job was to be done, as well as what tools and materials were to be used for the job. Sixty-three (35 per cent) of the previous jobs either generally or entirely restricted the worker in these respects. At Plant X, almost all jobs, with only a handful of exceptions, were restricted. This means that over 100 workers experienced a sharp change with respect to this factor.

We have now looked at the previous jobs of the assembly line workers at Plant X and compared them with their present ones in regard to origin of pace, repetitiveness, skill, and the choice of tools and techniques. There remains another important question relative to the immediate content of the job. Does a man work on the entire or on a substantial portion of the product or service, or does he work on only a minute fraction? For all but a handful of the jobs on the assembly line, the men worked on a minute fractional unit of the automobile. Of previous jobs, eighty-four (46.6 per cent) were such that a man worked on a substantial portion of the product or service. Ninety-two (51.1 per cent) worked on a fraction of the product or service.

To sum up: In the Introduction we listed six basic characteristics of automobile assembly work: mechanical pacing of work (by moving conveyors), repetitiveness, minimum skill requirement, predetermination in use of tools and techniques, minute subdivision of product worked on, and surface mental attention. The workers interviewed indicated that with regard to the first five characteristics they had undergone a drastic change in work experience through shifting from their previous jobs to work in Plant X.*

---

* No *direct* comments were sought on surface mental attention. This element is somewhat difficult to measure, and comparisons based in part upon recollections were found to be unsatisfactory. A study of job descriptions and of unsolicited comments on fatigue suggests (1) the demand for mental attention appeared greater on the present job as compared with previous jobs; (2) more than half of the workers appeared to find their present jobs more fatiguing than their previous ones. Our data are insufficient, however, to show in each case whether this fatigue was mainly due to boredom and tension or to physical effort.

4 THE IMMEDIATE JOB

Taken together, Plant X jobs exemplify all the characteristics of automobile assembly work, but not every job exemplifies all of them. Put another way, in spite of many common characteristics, automobile assembly jobs are far from being equal, either in the quantity or quality of job content, or in the satisfaction or dissatisfaction which workers derive from that content. They differ both in the number of the several assembly line characteristics they exemplify and in the degree of impact of any one characteristic. An understanding of this point must mark the beginning of any serious inquiry into the relation of human behavior to assembly line work.

To give some simple illustrations: A job requiring the performance of five simple operations is repetitive, but to a lesser degree than a job requiring a single operation. The jobs of the fifty-seven men in our sample who performed a single operation were more repetitive than those of the 123 who performed two or more operations.* Thus, contrary to the common view of those who think of all assembly line jobs as equally repetitive and machine-controlled, or unskilled and monotonous, and so forth, there are important differences well understood by and vitally important to the assembly worker. Before recording worker attitudes we shall look at these differences.

The central factor in the immediate job experience of most workers is their relation to the main line. The reason has been suggested earlier: the moving conveyor chiefly determines work

* An "operation" is here defined as being a series of motions by the worker which are generally concerned with the use of the same tool, and generally applied to the same part of a product.

pace. From this standpoint, then, there are three main types of jobs — assembly jobs on the main line, sub-assembly jobs off the main line but on a moving feeder belt or conveyor, and sub-assembly jobs off the line and not on a moving belt or conveyor.

In describing their jobs a large number of workers made these relational distinctions and described how they felt about being on the line, off the line, at a bench, and so forth. These distinctions were brought out very clearly by the few men who had moved from on-the-line to off-the-line jobs. From the standpoint of pace, we can add a fourth subclassification: on the line but not governed by its pace. A repairman finishes his repair job if he can; if not, it is completed at a later time in the assembly sequence by another worker. The repairmen interviewed stressed this point.

There are other differences with regard to pace and to the line. On certain jobs, by increasing speed of individual performance, men can "work their way back up the line" a distance of four or five cars or four or five unit assemblies. Then for a few minutes, until the line catches up with them, they can take a "spell." Thus they acquire an element of control over pace plus a brief rest period.

Not all jobs permit this pace variation. Working back is impossible when a man cannot start doing his job until a preceding preparatory operation has been completed by the worker immediately before him. Another situation which may prevent it occurs where necessary tools or equipment are stationary and can only be used in a limited area. Finally, working back is difficult when too many operations are assigned to a man in a given time cycle or when the conveyor pace is stepped up, a phenomenon popularly known as the "speed up."

Thus, pace differences as set by the moving line occur in accordance with whether jobs are: (1) assembly jobs on the main line; (2) sub-assembly jobs off the main line but on a moving belt or conveyor; (3) sub-assembly jobs off the main line but not on a moving belt or conveyor; or (4) repair jobs on main or sub-assembly lines.

Turning now to repetitiveness, it has already been suggested that there are appreciable differences in the degree of repetitiveness in assembly jobs, and the simplest reason why certain jobs are more varied, or less repetitive, than others is that they have a larger number of distinct operations.

Table 4 breaks down the jobs of the 180 men interviewed in terms of number of operations. From this table it is clear that 121 men had jobs containing not more than five operations; twenty-nine men had jobs of from five to ten; and twenty-eight

TABLE **4**

Operations Performed on Immediate Job

Number of Operations	Number of Men	Per Cent of Sample
1	57	31.7
2	23	12.8
3–5	41	22.8
5–10	29	16.1
10 or more	28	15.5
Indeterminate	2	1.1
Total	180	100.0

had over ten operations. Generally speaking, *as the number of operations increases, the factor of "variety of job content" increases.*

Variety also derives from other causes such as the nature of the work (repair work) and differences in the product (model and make).* To illustrate how differences in product contribute to variety: to perform a particular operation on a convertible coupe at times requires a different set of parts or motions or both than does the same type of operation on a four-door sedan. This limited type of variety applies to three-quarters of the assembly line jobs in Plant X.

Frequent transfer among jobs brings variety to a limited number of workers known as "utilitymen." The utilityman must know

* In certain industrial processes variety is introduced into the workers' jobs through the differences in the materials employed. For example, metallurgical differences introduce variety into certain metal-working occupations.

every job in his section so that he can fill in when a man is absent from work or spell him if he wishes to leave the line for a few minutes. We shall quote presently the job description given by a utilityman who had been trained to perform twenty-eight different jobs. In comparison with the bulk of workers, the utilitymen have jobs with great variety in them, but that variety is clearly different from the variety of a repairman's job. It is derived from frequent transfer among repetitive jobs rather than from the varied nature of the work on an individual job.

Variety on assembly jobs is gained, then, through (1) a large number of operations; (2) the nature of the work, such as that of repairmen; (3) frequent transfer from one job to another, such as that of utilitymen; and (4) variety of makes and models.

So much for our first two characteristics of assembly line work, mechanical pacing and repetitiveness. We turn now to *minimum skill requirement*. Skills, in the traditional sense of skills of hand or brain associated with craft, are notably absent from automobile assembly work. On the other hand, there are no unskilled labor jobs on an assembly line. *The Dictionary of Occupational Titles* solves the problem of definition quite inadequately by classifying nearly all automobile assemblers' jobs as semiskilled. Semiskilled in what sense? A few of these "semiskilled" jobs require many months to learn, others only a few hours; yet both appear under the same classification. Clearly the difficulty stems from the basic differences between mass production jobs and manufacturing jobs at the time the "skilled, semiskilled, unskilled" categories came into being.

Almost all mass production jobs, including the common run of automobile assembly line jobs, do not call for skill in the sense of judgment, experience, and varied dexterity of eye and hand. Quite often, however, they do call for a great deal of concentrated practice to assure easy and accurate performance. "Practice" and "knack" appear to be the appropriate words, then, rather than "skill." In some cases the knack can be quickly acquired in a few days; in other cases it takes several months. For the bulk of assembly jobs we shall use learning time as our chief measure of skill.

At least four classifications may be distinguished in an ascending order of complexity of skills. First come the single-operation jobs, requiring only the ability to repeat a simple cycle of motions at a given pace, such as putting in screws and tightening them with an air-driven screwdriver.

Second, there are jobs with three to five operations on one or several different parts. Thus a man might insert a set of screws in one metal plate, fit clips to another, and drill holes in a third. All these jobs can be learned in from a day to a week, depending on the simplicity of the operations and the worker's aptitude.

In a third and somewhat special category are the jobs of utility-men, whose very substantial skill is the sum of the skills or knacks of many more routine jobs.

In the fourth category come the few jobs which more nearly require the exercise of skills in the conventional sense. The repair-man's job is an example, as is that of the dingman. The latter "dings" out surface imperfections on the body of a car in accordance with contour specifications with a series of special-headed hammers. It takes the dingman several months of learning time to acquire this skill. In addition, there are some jobs for which the mastery of a skilled trade is required. Even so, because auto assembly jobs are standardized, the worker exercises a minimum number of his special abilities. Examples are the spot and arc welders' jobs. Skills, then may be classified as follows: (1) single operation jobs requiring a day to a week of learning time; (2) three to five operation jobs requiring a day to a week of learning time; (3) the jobs of utilitymen, whose skills are the sum of a number of low-skilled jobs, each of which requires a day to a week of learning time; and (4) the jobs of repairmen and a few others, who exercise skills of eye and hand and judgment in the traditional trade or craft sense.

The fourth characteristic of assembly line work is *predetermination* in the use *of tools and techniques*. Since this applies to all assembly jobs with the exception of repair work, it needs no further discussion. Similarly for the fifth, *minute subdivision of product* worked on: this, too, applies to all jobs except those of repairmen and utilitymen. As regards the sixth characteristic, *surface mental attention*, there are unquestionably small variations from job to job which are of significance to the individual. Our data, however, are not sufficient to justify a refined analysis. Clearly, this characteristic like the preceding two is not applicable to repairmen.

A comment is appropriate at this point on the physical energy required by assembly line jobs. In spite of the great strides taken toward the full mechanization of automotive assembly lines, including overhead trolleys, powered hand tools, electric lifts, and other laborsaving devices, considerable muscular energy is still demanded of the assembly line workers. Roughly, there are three kinds of jobs in terms of energy expenditure: (1) light, where the operator handles small parts, as in the installation of handles and locks; (2) medium, where the operator installs such parts as steering columns; and (3) heavy, where the operator must lift heavy parts such as wheels or doors, or must manipulate heavy tools.

Our interviews with workers were divided roughly into three parts. We asked each worker to describe his job; we asked him a number of questions about all the major elements in his total job situation; and we asked him to give a comparative rating in terms of likes and dislikes to these several elements. In order to clarify our analysis of assembly line characteristics, we shall turn briefly to this interview material for illustrations of assembly jobs in the workers' own words. We shall also draw upon material from the rating scales to show how the workers discriminated among the characteristics. (The construction of the rating scale is briefly described on page 61, fully described in Appendix A.)

The jobs chosen include (1) two assembly jobs on the main moving line, (2) one off the main line but on a moving conveyor, (3) one off the main line but not on a moving conveyor, (4) one repair job on the line, and (5) one utility job on the line. These six will concretize most of the job differences we have been discussing.

(1) *On the main moving line.* Here is the way the assembler of the baffle windbreaker in the Trim Department describes his job:

As the body shell moves along the line, I start putting on a baffle windbreaker (two fenders fit on it) by putting in four screws. Then I put nine clips at the bottom which hold the chrome molding strip to the body. On another type of car there is a piece of rubber which fits on the hood latch on the side and keeps the hood from rattling. I drill the holes in the rubber and metal and fit two screws in. Also, I put four clips on the rubber in the rear fender.

On another type of body, I put the clips on the bottom molding, and in the trunk space I put two bolts which hold the spare tire clamp. I repeat these things all the time on the same types of car.

Now look at this man's job in terms of pace, variety, and skill, three of the characteristics we have been analyzing. To begin with, the job is on the main line and the worker rides along on the conveyor, completing his cycle of operations in less than two minutes while the conveyor is moving over a distance of about thirty feet. He then walks to his starting point and begins over again. In short, his pace is directly determined by the moving belt. On the other hand, he is sometimes able to work back up the line and so secure a breather for himself.

As for variety, the job is clearly repetitive, but there is some element af variety since between five and ten operations are required to complete the job cycle. There are also different models to be worked on. Comparing the repetitiveness of this job with that of other assembly jobs, it is somewhere in the middle range: far less repetitive than a single-operation job, far more repetitive than the job of a repairman.

Similarly, in the matter of skill, it is in the middle as assembly line jobs go. Because of the number of parts handled, learning time is slightly longer than that for many assembly jobs. The worker reported that it took him a month to learn to do the job properly. As for the expenditure of physical energy, it is a light job.

In the worker's own summary of what he liked about his whole job, he listed the good pay, steady work, and good working hours — in that order. He also checked "have interesting work" and "do many different things." In explanation of "interesting," he said, "It is fairly interesting, something new for me. I never owned a car, and I never worked on one before." He disliked the job because it was physically tiring,* because he could not set his own pace, and because the plant was too far away from his home.

The worker who installs toe plates performs operations typical of short-cycle, on-the-main-line jobs:

I put in the two different toe-plates. They cover the holes where the brake and clutch pedals are. I am inside the car and have to be down on the seat to do my work. On one kind of car I put in the shift lever while another man puts in the toe plates.

While doing his job this man rides along in the car and must complete the job before he is carried too far. After finishing his work cycle, he returns to his station, climbs into another car, and begins another installation. Thus his pace is strictly governed by the moving line. This particular worker told the interviewer that he did not mind the pace.

Such a job, which demands but two operations in a two-minute cycle, is highly repetitive. Only slight variety is introduced when the man installs a shift lever instead of a toe plate on certain cars.

The job demands very little skill and has a learning period of just two days. Although the worker gets in and out of cars twenty or thirty times an hour, his expenditure of physical energy on the actual assembly operation is slight.

(2) *Off the main line but on a moving conveyor.* We turn now

---

* Men who performed light work, as in the case of this worker, often said that the job was physically tiring. They generally explained that while the operations did not require excessive muscular energy, the job for other reasons (pacing, and so forth) was exhausting.

to a seat spring builder whose job is typical of those off the main line but on a moving belt:

I work on a small conveyor which goes around in a circle. We call it a "merry-go-round." I make up zigzag springs for front seats. Every couple of feet on the conveyor there is a form for the pieces that make up the seat springs. As that form goes by me, I clip several pieces together, using a clip gun. I then put the pieces back on the form, and it goes on around to where other men clip more pieces together. By the time the form has gone around the whole line, the pieces are ready to be set in a frame, where they are made into a complete seat spring. That's further down the main seat cushion line. The only operation I do is work the clip gun. It takes just a couple of seconds to shoot six or eight clips onto the spring, and I do it as I walk a few steps. Then I start right over again.

This job is clearly paced by a moving conveyor quite as much as if it were on the main line. A comment by the worker regarding his previous job emphasized the point: "I like the piecework system on my old job. If I wanted to stop for a few minutes I could. You can't do that here."

As for variety, there is none. The job is highly repetitive, consisting of one set of operations repeated every few seconds on a part which is standard for all models.

The skill requirement is minimum. This worker gave two days as his learning time, with a few days more "in order to do it like I do it now."

As for physical energy, the job would probably be rated as light, since the worker guides an automatic hand gun. But there is considerable fatigue because the operation is performed by the worker in a standing position.

The worker's over-all estimate of the job is typical. On the like side of the rating scale he listed good pay, steady work, and good working hours in this order of priority. On the dislike side he checked "could not set my own pace," "do not have interesting work," and "physically tiring."

(3) *Off the main line but not on a moving conveyor.* We turn to a blower-defroster assembler who works off the main line and not on a moving belt:

I work at a bench on blower-defrosters. The blowers come in two parts. I take one part and attach the blower motor to it. I then connect the fan to the motor shaft. Then I take the other half of the air pipe and put two parts together with fourteen screws. I test the motor to see if it works, and if it does, I put in a fifteenth screw which grounds it to the pipe.

The materials are brought to me and put in a pile by a stock chaser. After I finish, I put each assembled blower on one of six shelves.

Here is an example of a job where pace is only indirectly determined by the main line. The worker must keep his shelves stocked with a supply of completed blower-defrosters, but he has some choice of pace in doing so. He may work fast and build up a full supply, then slow down and take a breather. Or he may choose to work quite steadily. The demands of the stock-chaser who brings him materials and takes away the finished assembly are the determinants of his work pace, rather than the moving conveyor.

There is not much variety, since there are only three operations. However, slight variations are introduced through differences in models. The worker called his job completely repetitive, but said he did not mind it.

His job operations require a minimum of skill: "I learned it in a couple of hours, but it took me about a week to get up speed." He does not move around, and the materials he handles are light, so very little physical energy is demanded.

Summing up his job, this worker gave good bosses, good pay, and good working conditions as the first three reasons for liking his job. He mentioned only one item in the dislike column: "Cannot do different things."

(4) *Repairman.* We turn to the job of a repairman in the car conditioning section of the Chassis Department:

I work in a pit underneath the final line. The cars move along over the pit. On the previous assembly operations, the inspectors for the under parts of the car have indicated where parts were missing or damaged or not properly attached. There are any number of things which can be wrong, and they are usually different for each car. Sometimes we have a run of the same thing which we have to work on until they get at the bug earlier in assembly operations. The shock absorbers may be bad, gas line in wrong, brakes lines, spring attachments off. I fix whatever I see checked by the inspector. The others in the pit do the same thing. I just work down the line until I get it cleared up. Sometimes I have to work down a long way on one thing. Other times it's just a simple problem on a number of different things.

This worker is on the main line, but his pace is not strictly governed by the moving conveyor. "We don't feel the pressure of the line, since we don't have to do just one thing in a given area and length of time."

The variety the job offers is derived from the nature of the work. "There are any number of things which can be wrong, and they are usually different for each car . . . There is something different all the time."

As for skill, the job as repairman requires manual skill and mechanical experience. A garage repairman's job would be a good preparation.* When asked how long it had taken him to learn his job well enough to keep up with the others, this particular repairman replied, "I had done it before. I've fooled around with cars since I was twelve. It would take a year for a new fellow, I guess."

The job calls for a varying expenditure of physical energy and changes appreciably from job to job and from day to day between light and medium heavy work.

The worker's personal satisfaction with his job showed up clearly on the rating scale. In the dislike column there were no items marked. On the other hand, he gave as his first three rea-

---

* The man whose job description is given here had, in fact, worked as a repairman in a garage before coming to Plant X.

sons for liking the job "set my own pace, good working conditions, and steady work," respectively. He also marked in the like column "have interesting work, have to use my brains, do many different things, can talk with others, can work alone, can move around on the job," and "can choose how the job is to be done."

(5) *Utilityman*. A utilityman in the Chassis Department describes his job as follows:

I work on the whole length of that part of the chassis line, beginning with motor drop up to where the wheels are mounted. My job is to fill in wherever I am needed. A man might be absent or away from the job or may need help on the job.

We start where the motor is lowered onto the frame (motor mount). The clutch assembly is installed and hooked up. Then the exhaust system is attached and the bolts tightened. The clutch assembly bolts and the motor mount bolts are also tightened. In the next area on the line the brake chambers are filled and bled.

Off to the side, the sub-assembly men put the steering column together. The steering post and the Pittman arm assembly are put in. Further down the line, men put in air cleaners and inject hydraulic fluid for the transmission. Next the brakes are tested and the clutch linkage hooked up. The bumper brackets are put on, a serial number is attached next, and then the bumper brackets are tightened up. Finally the chassis is sprayed, mounted on wheels, and moved on toward body drop. All in all, about twenty-eight men work on these jobs, each man with his own special operation. I go on each of these jobs, depending on where I am needed most. It is different each day. Some of the jobs are hard to learn, so when I take over one on which I haven't had much experience, it's hard to keep up. I have been learning how to do the work ever since I've been in the plant. I can never learn everything because new changes are always being made.

The pace of this utilityman's work, since it is on the main line, is as strictly governed as that of any assembly worker. In certain ways he may feel the pressure more acutely than some of those for whom he substitutes, since he has less practice on any single job than its regular holder.

To compensate, however, there is plenty of variety, since, as he points out, he shifts about among twenty-eight different jobs.

Notice how in describing his many tasks this utilityman gives a very clear account of a whole segment of assembly operations in the Chassis Department.

We have already made the point as to the nature of a utilityman's skill. It is the sum of many little skills of many repetitive jobs. The learning time is six months to a year. The worker said: "Sometimes I walk up and down checking the line. I ask questions of the different men. I rarely stay on the same job more than a couple of days." That his job is not easy is suggested by an additional comment: "Some days you feel like learning, other days you don't. On jobs that take time to learn, you get disgusted because it's hard to keep up. A utilityman, when on a job, has more trouble keeping up than the regular man."

This man mentioned good pay, steady work, and good bosses as the three main reasons for liking his job, in that order. Other items in the like column of the rating scale bearing on the immediate job which he checked were "having interesting work, have to use my brains, do many different things," and "can talk with others." He checked only one item in the dislike column — "physically tiring."

In all of this classification of the automotive assembly workers' jobs, we have clearly been concerned not with an engineering analysis, but with factors which have an effect on satisfaction or dissatisfaction with the immediate job. Mechanical pace, repetitiveness, minimum skill requirement, and the other job characteristics were all found reflected in attitudes and feelings. These component origins of attitudes are quite concrete, and most of them can be expressed in terms either of a space-time relationship or of quantity.

II

We turn now from this over-all breakdown of assembly line jobs and their characteristics to what the assembly worker thought or felt about them. Naturally, each worker's reaction to his immediate job differed somewhat from that of every other worker, both because of the nature of the particular job and because of personality differences. Nevertheless, on many points there were significant groupings of attitude.

Before setting down these reactions, it is worth pointing to the main distribution of jobs in our sample of 180 men:

Main assembly line	86	47.8%
Sub-assembly on moving belt	28	15.5%
Sub-assembly not on moving belt	38	21.1%
Repairmen	14	7.8%
Utilitymen	11	6.1%
Other	3	1.7%

We asked no direct attitude questions on the first and central characteristic of an automobile assembly plant, the moving conveyor, but nearly every worker expressed his opinions about this characteristic, either when describing his job, when talking about the company, or at some other point in the interview. These free association comments on pace as governed by the moving conveyor showed that (1) a large majority of the workers regarded the moving line or belt as an undesirable feature of the job; and (2) a small minority expressed themselves as enjoying the excitement of the moving line.

The bad thing about assembly lines is that the line keeps moving. If you have a little trouble with a job, you can't take the time to do it right.

On the line you're geared to the line. You don't dare stop. If you get behind, you have a hard time catching up.

The line speed is too great. More men wouldn't help much. They'd just expect more work out of an individual. There's an awful lot of tension.

I don't like rushing all the time . . . I don't mind doing a good day's work, but I don't like to run through it.

The work isn't hard, it's the never-ending pace . . . The guys yell "hurrah" whenever the line breaks down . . . you can hear it all over the plant.

Some of the workers complained equally of pace and monotony. A greater number, however, made a distinction between the two and were more critical of pace than of monotony:

It's not the monotony, it's the rush, rush, rush.

The line speed is too fast . . . The work isn't monotonous . . . It's very interesting because I see all the different kinds of jobs around me.

I'd like my job if they didn't rush me all the time. I'd hate to have my boy work like this.

In contrast, a minority liked the challenge and excitement of keeping up with the line:

I do my job well. I get some satisfaction from keeping up with a rapid-fire job. On days when the cars come off slowly, I sometimes get bored.

I get satisfaction from doing my job right and keeping up with the line.

There's too much rush for the manpower to get quality. It makes you feel good, though, when the line is going like hell and you step in and catch it up.

We turn now to repetitiveness versus variety and workers' comments on these points. On the basis of questions concerning jobs men had *before* they came to the automobile plant, two important facts were revealed: (1) most of the previous jobs had considerably more variety than did present jobs; (2) job satisfaction was related to variety.

These facts may be demonstrated in Table 5. In discussing his previous job, the respondent was asked: "Some people like to do the same thing over and over again on their jobs, and others do not. Thinking about the particular job you had before coming to Plant X, how do you stand?" The answers were then compared with repetitiveness or nonrepetitiveness as determined by analysis of job descriptions.

The results shown in Table 5 clearly indicate that men who had nonrepetitive jobs liked the varied nature of their work, and that those whose jobs were repetitive disliked that aspect of the job.

Contrasted with former jobs, most Plant X jobs were, as we have seen, highly repetitive. Workers' attitudes on the question of variety versus repetition had not measurably changed. They

TABLE **5**

Repetitive and Nonrepetitive Work as Factors in Liking or Not Liking Previous Jobs

	Repetitive Job	Non-repetitive Job	Total
Liked	13	109	122
No difference	6	6	12
Disliked	28	6	34
Total	47	121	168

$x^2 = 70.93$ $n = 2$ $P < .001$

still disliked repetitive work. Of the workers interviewed, 85 per cent said they *preferred* to perform different operations, 8 per cent said they liked repetitive work, and the remaining 7 per cent said it made no difference.

Despite the repetitive nature of Plant X jobs in general, certain distinctions within the jobs were noted. Some workers repeated a single operation continuously throughout the work day. Others repeated several operations within their prescribed job cycle. In an attempt to relate the number of operations to job satisfaction, correlations were made between operations and the question: "Would you say your job was very interesting, fairly interesting, not too interesting, or not at all interesting?" The results are shown in Table 6. In this table it is clearly shown that as the number of operations increases, workers were more likely to call their jobs "interesting." Those with fewer operations to perform reflected a negative interest in their jobs.

As in the case of pacing, perhaps the most valuable data on attitude toward repetitiveness versus variety came from unsolicited comments scattered through the interviews. Taken as a whole they reveal chiefly that (1) a majority of the workers were critical of the repetitive character of their jobs; (2) a minority preferred the repetitive character of their work or were indifferent to it; and (3) a large number of workers compared on-the-line jobs unfavorably with off-the-line jobs, because off-the-line jobs offered more variety.

TABLE **6**

Operations Performed Correlated with Degree of Job Interest, Present Job

Operations Performed	Very or Fairly Interesting	Not Very or Not At All Interesting	Total
1	19	38	57
2–5	28	36	64
5 or more	41	18	59
Total	88	92	180

$x^2 = 16.23$ $n = 2$ $P < .001$

Following are typical comments of those men who were critical of the repetitive nature of their jobs:

I dislike repetition. One of the main things wrong with this job is that there is no figuring for yourself; no chance to use my brain. It's a grind doing the same thing over and over. There is no skill necessary.

I'd rather work for a small company any day. They're interested in doing good work, and they are willing to allot enough time for it. The assembly line is no place to work, I can tell you. There is nothing more discouraging than having a barrel beside you with 10,000 bolts in it and using them all up. Then you get a barrel with another 10,000 bolts, and you know every one of those 10,000 bolts has to be picked up and put in exactly the same place as the last 10,000 bolts.

I'd like to do different things on this job. I get bored. It's the same thing all the time. Cars always coming down the line endlessly every time I look up.

I'd like to do more things. That's the trouble with the line. Monotony. You repeat the same thing day in, day out.

I would like to perform different operations, but I do the same thing all the time. I always know what I'm going to do when I come in. There's nothing to look forward to like there was on my old job.

The monotony is what I don't like. It's pretty noisy, but you get used to that. I'd never get used to the monotony. I dislike the plant for this reason.

It's not a matter of pace. It's the monotony. It's not good for you to get so bored. I do the same thing day after day; just an everlasting grind.

The job gets so sickening — day in and day out plugging in ignition wires. I get through with one motor, turn around, and there's another motor staring me in the face. It's sickening.

A minority of workers who declared that they were indifferent to or preferred doing the same thing over and over again commented as follows:

I keep doing the same thing all the time, but it doesn't make any difference to me.

Repeating the same thing you can catch up and keep ahead of yourself. I like the routine. You can get in the swing of it.

We do the same thing all the time, but I don't mind it really.

I repeat the same thing day in and day out. I like it — I can do it fast.

I like doing the same thing all the time. I'd rather stay right where I am. When I come in in the morning, I like to know exactly what I'll be doing.

I like to repeat the same thing, and every car is different anyway. So my job is interesting enough.

Explanation of why this minority group either preferred or was indifferent to the factor of repetitiveness in contrast to the majority of workers in our sample would appear to lie in the pattern of their individual personalities. An investigation of personalities in this group is clearly suggested. We sought but found no other unique characteristics in this group as regards education, age, or our other categories of information.

A number of workers made sharp comparisons between jobs on and off the main line as regards monotony and pace.

I would like to perform different operations, but my job is better than most. It's not on the line; I'm not tied to the line like most.

My job is different every day. I wouldn't want to have a regular line job. Not as much pay and not the chance to improve yourself.

I like to be doing different things. That's why I took the job, to get off the line.

I move cars around. I perform quite a few things, actually. There's enough variety to satisfy me. It's not like turning a screw all day on the production line.

I can do most anything on my job. It's not as monotonous as that of most guys. I do the job of anybody who is out or in the hole. I'm sort of assistant foreman. I also fill in when the foreman tells me a guy wants to take a break.

I prefer a job off the line. Mine is pretty good because I don't have to keep up with the line. When I was on the line, I thought I was back in the Army. Just regimentation. You're like a big army, and the foremen are master sergeants. Off the line, work is not a steady grind, routine and monotonous. On my job, for example, I rarely do the same thing twice. I repair different things because the same mistakes aren't always made on the wiring. If they do get routine, I go to the foreman or the operator and tell him what mistake he's making all the time. The foreman leaves it to me to stop these installation mistakes.

Although nearly all workers remarked on both pace and repetitiveness, many also touched, directly or indirectly, on the other characteristics of assembly line jobs. The third characteristic, minimum skill requirement, came in for considerable comment. Here are representative remarks made by those whose jobs required little skill:

Ten minutes — any junior high school kid could do it — except he wouldn't.

Only took a half hour to pick it up — then it's only a question of speeding up. Some men get it in less than half an hour.

You can learn any of the jobs in two hours.

Two hours — nothing to learn.

Learned the job in a couple of hours.

Took a week to get up speed.

A five-year old can come in and do it now.

It took approximately three days on-the-job training. No previous work experience was of any value learning this job.

Most workers on the jobs with the least learning time were like the above, inclined to be apologetic or a little ashamed. As learning time increased, the tone of apology disappeared, and in some cases a touch of pride entered into the comments:

Worker who put balls in fly-wheel assembly and tests them for tension: At least a month to learn. It takes quite a while to get real savvy on the job. And it takes some practice to know how to tongue bolts and get them at the right tension.

Metal finisher: I went to school two weeks — then on to line. Took about three months before I could keep up with it.

Worker who removes dents from hoods: Each hood is different for every car. Took me six months to learn it. And it takes years to be good at it.

Final repair worker: I'm still learning. And a new model will be coming soon. A repairman just about really learns everything about the job on one model when a new one comes in. It took me a couple of months to catch on, but I knew something about metal and maybe that helped a bit.

Polisher: Takes about three months to get by but a year to learn it right.

Utilityman: I was there seven months before I got on to it.

In comparing previous to present jobs, a good many workers said they had greater freedom in the way they did their jobs before they came to Plant X. This was an indirect comment upon the fourth characteristic of assembly line work, predetermination in use of tools and techniques.

A few workers also commented directly on the fifth characteristic, minute subdivision of product worked on. Here is a an example:

When the plant was running only a few cars through an hour, I used to install the whole front and back seat assemblies. But when the cars speeded up, I was put on the job of installing the rack that the front seat slides back and forth on, and my job was broken up and simplified. I'd like to do a whole fender myself from raw material to the finished job. It would be more interesting.

The sixth characteristic, surface attention, was not specifically commented upon, but is deducible for almost all jobs from the nature of the jobs themselves as disclosed in the job descriptions. As to the amount of physical effort required, "physically tiring" registered second on the rating scale as a reason for disliking the immediate job at Plant X.

It should be recalled that an important minority of workers found their immediate jobs on or off the lines thoroughly satisfactory. These included all the repairmen and utilitymen interviewed with the exception of one. Besides this group, however, there were also production workers who favored their immediate jobs for the following reasons:

(1) Social interaction breaking the monotony.

(2) Enough operations on their particular jobs to give variety.

(3) Ability to work back up the line and get a breather.

(4) Ability to build up a bank and get a breather.

(5) Ability to alternate one set of operations with another set of a substantially different character.

(6) Ability to alternate jobs with other workers within the same section.

(7) A long time cycle encompassing a larger number of operations than usual and of a more interesting character.

In the conclusion of this inquiry the question will be raised as to the extent to which these particular job characteristics could be spread more widely through an automobile assembly plant.

When commenting on features of the immediate job in preliminary interviews, workers frequently related job satisfaction to the quality of work performed. Allowance was, therefore, made in the final schedule of questions for further exploration of the question of satisfaction and quality.

Seventy-nine men in the sample of 180 felt that it was difficult to sustain the kind of quality performance which was expected of them or which they themselves wanted to sustain. To most of the seventy-nine this was a discouraging and negative feature of the job. Such reactions were generally found among those whose jobs were strictly line paced.

Slightly over half of the workers (ninety-five) considered that it was usually possible to achieve "good quality work" on their jobs. Typical comments among this group were:

We put out good quality. My job is done right. They don't fool with what I've done after I've finished.

No time limit is set on my job, so I can do it right. I get satisfaction out of really fixing a job. I can usually get this, but sometimes the company doesn't want the cars fixed as well as I'd like to.

I get satisfaction and quality because I have time to complete my job right.

I like doing a nice paint job. I feel good about it. Sometimes I'm rushed, but I can usually get some satisfaction from the job I do.

I never let a car go by with my number on it unless it is done right. Maybe some of the men on the line don't get quality.

You can take time to get quality. It's not like on the line when you have to rush so much. And I get work satisfaction. It makes me feel good when I put out a good day's work and get no kickbacks.

If they rush us we can't get too good quality. You scratch panels, et cetera. We used to be too rushed, but now we rearranged the job and get some satisfaction out of the job.

My job is very interesting because it's very important. If I don't get the windows (installed) right, it messes everything up. They count on me to get them right; if the windows are not right, they want to know why.

The effects of poor quality work on job satisfaction are shown in the remarks below:

You cannot get quality and quantity. That's my big worry about the place. I don't like it. I always liked to be proud of my work. But I can't be on this job very much. Everyone is working under too much pressure for speed and "get it out."

The cars come too fast for quality. It's quantity instead of quality. I'm doing the best I can, but could do a neater job slower.

On an assembly line you just do it once; if it's wrong, you have no time to fix it. I get no satisfaction from my work. All I do is think about all the things that went through wrong that should have been fixed. My old job was nothing like this.

I try to do quality work, but I'm too rushed. This keeps me from getting pleasure from the work. They say, "haste makes waste," and they're getting plenty of both.

I can't do a job without doing it good and properly. But I get no satisfaction from this job; I get no feeling like that. I wish I could. It would make the job more pleasant. I've had work satisfaction on my other jobs.

I'd rather do less work and do it right. How can you get quality when they don't give you time? The "quality" signs they have mean nothing.

These comments tend to show that all or most of the characteristics or components of the assembly man's immediate job have some bearing upon the quality of the product. Although restricting it, mass production methods did not eliminate the "human factor" as a determinant of quality for any given part or for the total product. Most workers were conscious of this fact. For a substantial number, inability to put out quality was a source of irritation, putting out quality a source of job satisfaction.

III

The comments which we have been quoting give a general idea of workers' reactions to the immediate content of their jobs. But they do not tell how much comparative weight or value the average worker was putting on this or that factor. For example, consider the several components or mass production characteristics of the immediate job. Did the average worker think mechanical pacing more important or less important than repetitiveness to his feelings about his job? Or take what we have called "elements" in the total job picture at Plant X: relations with other workers, pay and security, relations with supervision, general working conditions, and the others. How did the production worker rate his immediate job in comparison with these other essential elements?

In order to secure an answer to such questions, a rating scale was devised.* In preliminary interviews we noted down those subjects connected with the job which appeared of most importance to the workers. From these were drawn up a list of fifty-two items recorded in the actual words and phrases used by workers. Half of these items were favorable expressions about various elements in the total job. The other half, their counterparts, were unfavorable. The range of topics covered many aspects of the job elements — immediate job content, relations with supervision, fellow workers, pay, the union, promotion, and so forth. In the regular series of interviews each worker was asked to check the items on the list which were important as reasons for liking his job and which were important for his not liking it. Using the results of this rating, we now turn to our two questions:

(1) What comparative ratings were given by the worker to the several components *within* his immediate job experience?

* The reader will remember that we drew briefly on material from this rating scale on p. 43 to fill out the half dozen worker descriptions of specific jobs. For a full description and discussion, see Appendix A, p. 171.

(2) What comparative ratings did he give to the immediate job in comparison with other elements in the total job picture at Plant X?

Within immediate job experience, the factor of mechanical pacing received the top rating as a *dislike* factor. Here are the first five dislike items checked in order of importance by the workers: (1) cannot set my own pace; (2) physically tiring; (3) do not have interesting work; (4) cannot do different things; and (5) cannot use my brains.

In terms of our general definitions, then, those characteristics of assembly line work which appeared of greatest importance as unfavorable features of the immediate job were mechanical pacing of work, repetitiveness, and minimum skill.

Figure 2 shows an interesting and striking contrast of worker attitudes toward immediate job factors at Plant X compared with worker attitudes toward the same factors on previous jobs. Notice that on previous jobs the favorable aspects of immediate job content far outranked the unfavorable features, but that this rating was reversed when the same workers considered their present jobs.

The statistics used in constructing Figure 2 show that only seven men put an immediate job factor as the primary reason for liking their assembly jobs. Of these, five were utility or repairmen; in other words, men whose jobs embodied both variety and skill. (Nineteen listed one factor, as the second, and twenty-eight gave one as the third reason.) In contrast, ninety-six workers singled out an immediate job factor, usually mechanical pacing, as the most important disliked feature of the job. (Eighty-two rated one of the immediate job factors as the second most disliked feature, and sixty rated one as the third.) This contrast was particularly marked in the qualitative comments of the workers.

Figure 2 and the statistics behind it are interesting in the light of the facts recorded in Chapter III, "From the Old Job to the New." There we showed that workers generally were experiencing a sharp change in immediate job experience when they came to

Plant X and that this change was received unfavorably by most of them.

We turn now to the second question: How did the worker rate his immediate job in comparison with other job elements in the total situation at Plant X? Our rating scale gives a fairly clear answer. In the like column, pay and security rate far above any

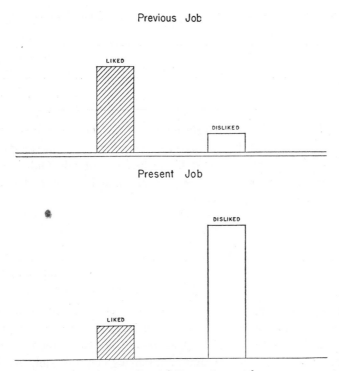

Fig. 2. Immediate Job Factors Compared.

single factor of the immediate job and all other elements. In the dislike column the immediate job heads the list. In other words, no other disliked feature meant as much to the workers as mechanical pacing, repetitiveness, and the related items comprising immediate job content.

When these ratings of the Plant X assembly job are compared

with ratings of the workers' previous jobs, the same type of contrast with which we have become familiar emerges. Table 7, for example, presents comparisons between pay and security, considered as a single economic element, and immediate job content. Clearly, former jobs were disliked for economic reasons and

TABLE **7**

Economic Elements and Immediate Job Content Ratings, Previous and Present Jobs

	Likes		Dislikes	
Elements	Previous	Present	Previous	Present
Economic (pay and security)	54	147	81	1
Immediate job content	53	7	18	96

liked because of the intrinsic nature of the jobs. The reverse is true for Plant X. Only one man considered an economic factor as the principal reason for not liking his present job. Only seven among the entire sample of 180 put an immediate job factor first as a reason for liking the job.

SUMMARY

(1) From the standpoint of the men, there are very important differences among jobs on an assembly line. Taken together, Plant X jobs exemplified all the principal characteristics of assembly line work, but not every job exemplified all of them.

(2) Many workers thought of their jobs from the standpoint of relationship to the main line. Thus there were jobs directly on the main line, jobs off the line but on a moving conveyor, jobs off the line but not on a conveyor, and repairmen on main or sub-assembly lines.

(3) The degree of repetitiveness varied according to the number of operations performed, the nature of the work, and other factors.

(4) Qualitative comments showed that a majority of the workers disliked the mechanical pacing and the repetitive charac-

ter of their jobs. A minority expressed themselves as preferring or indifferent to these two characteristics.

(5) A correlation existed between interest in work and the number of operations performed. Interest in work varied directly, indifference inversely, with the number of operations.

(6) For a substantial number, inability to put out quality was a source of irritation, putting out quality a source of job satisfaction.

(7) Within their immediate job experience workers rated in the following order the disliked characteristics of their jobs: mechanical pacing, repetitiveness, minimum skill.

(8) Within the total job situation, pay and security rated first in the like column of the rating scale, the immediate job first in the dislike column.

5 WORKERS AND THE SOCIAL GROUP

In recent years, beginning especially with the work of Elton Mayo, we have witnessed a growing interest in the dynamics of group relationships in manufacturing plants. It has been pointed out, and well documented, that a man's attitude toward his immediate tasks, his supervisors, his union, and the company are all measurably affected by the way in which he accepts, or is accepted by, the immediate group with which he works. Observers also document what the intelligent factory manager has long known: that a worker's productivity is often directly related to his role as a member of a work group. A man may be well paid, work under ideal plant conditions, have excellent foremen, and even feel that his particular job is worth while; but if he is not integrated into a work group, his interest in his work, which is often reflected in productivity, will be low.

Causes of poor adjustment to the group situation are manifold. The industrial sociologist usually includes nationality antagonisms, status and prestige conflicts, age and sex differences, and, of course, personality clashes. These may all be important, but too often overlooked is the fact that technology in any given operational unit may be the crucial factor in determining the character of social relationships for any individual or for a group of individuals. What is the effect of the technology of the assembly line on social relations in Plant X? *

* In our emphasis upon the technological factor in this instance, we do not wish to imply that nationality, status, age, and so forth, are not sometimes crucial in determining the social structure of work groups. Our evidence suggests, however, that because of certain circumstances they were perhaps of less importance in Plant X than in many factories. Throughout our inter-

We shall begin by looking at the size of work groups and at the amount and quality of social interaction which took place among the workers at Plant X. Later we will examine the structure of social groups as determined by the technological facts of the assembly line itself.

Workers were asked to describe the "social geography" of their jobs in terms of (1) the number of men comprising their immediate work group and (2) the amount of interaction they had with their fellow workers during the course of the day.

Twenty men worked alone or with one other worker. The group occurring most frequently was composed of from two to five men. Sixty-eight out of the 179 responding said that they worked in groups of this size. Fifty said they worked in groups of from five to ten, and forty-one were in groups of more than ten men.

Eighty men reported that they were in contact with others near them at least once every five minutes. Another eighty-two reported contact with at least one other person near them at least three times during the working day. Seventeen indicated that they had "rare" (or less frequent) contact with others.

As workers described the size of their work groups and the amount of interaction within them, they were encouraged to discuss in qualitative terms what the opportunity to talk with others, or the lack of that opportunity, meant to them on the job. In response to a general question, "Is the opportunity to talk or

---

viewing program, for example, we could find little evidence of nationality conflicts. This might be explained by the fact that almost all workers were at least second generation Americans living in an area of the country which had experienced a long period of assimilation. Conflicts likely to arise about status and prestige were also minimized, we believe, for two reasons: First, a majority of the production workers received similar wages, within narrow limits; and, second, the plant was new, and there was not the familiar problem of the "old-timers" versus the "newcomers." At the time of this study there were no sex differences, since all the production workers were men. As pointed out earlier, two-thirds of the men were under thirty-two years old, and less than one-tenth were over forty. Unquestionably there were antagonisms based on personality differences which we were unable to explore. It may be pointed out, however, that only rarely were there hints of serious conflict based on personality differences.

not talk with others a reason for liking or not liking your job?"
137 workers said that the chance to talk and joke with others
was one reason, although not necessarily the principal one, for
liking their present jobs. Thirty-nine said that it made no difference, and four said that their inability to talk with any other
worker was one reason for not liking the job.

Typical of the qualitative comments regarding the social
aspects of the job were the following:

I like to talk. Gives me a chance to take my mind off my work,
gives it a little brighter outlook.

Talking to the other fellows takes up the strain of the job. It
relieves the tension.

Talking sometimes makes the time go faster. There are some
days, of course, when nothing makes the time go fast.

I like to talk on the job because it breaks the monotony. We can
talk all we want so long as it doesn't interfere with doing the job.

If I couldn't talk to somebody, I'd be talking to myself.

If it weren't for talking and fooling, you'd go nuts.

Though the large majority made comments such as these, it
was apparent that some workers enjoyed much greater freedom
of social interaction than others. These variations may be explained by the technical requirements and surroundings of
particular jobs.

One obvious limiting factor was noise. At many places
throughout plant operations it was difficult, if not impossible, to
talk. In the Metal Department, for example, spot welding and
grinding operations were particularly noisy. At one point,
popularly referred to as "the jungle," several dozen hand operated
spot welding guns pounded along the sheet metal surfaces at
once. Equally noisy were those sections in which men used high-
speed grinding machines. In other departments workers operated
hand drilling machines, clip guns, and overhead pulleys, all of
which created loud and sustained sounds making normal talking
difficult.

Another factor tending to limit "free" social interaction was the close attention to work required by many jobs. Workers had to watch each motion carefully throughout their work cycle. Failure to do so sometimes meant that the work was not completed in the cycle, and they "got in the hole," as the men put it. Or failure to pay constant attention could create safety hazards, since many of the hand tools were potentially dangerous.

Here are a few typical comments made by men who spoke of the above factors as limiting talking on the job:

I never worked in a place so noisy. Hard to talk to anyone when you're spot welding. Can't get used to it.

You can't talk and put on door handles.

We usually are so damn busy we don't have time to talk.

I like to talk but we can't much. The stuff is sharp and we have to pay close attention. I'd rather have a job where I could relax and talk a little more.

These comments reflect some of the limitations to social interaction inherent in many of the jobs. But, as indicated above, half of the workers were able to talk with others constantly or frequently during the day.

Thus far we have indicated that interaction took place within groups of various sizes and in varying amounts, that talking on the job was possible, but often with limitations.

What appears of even greater significance to our inquiry is the relationship between the technological environment and the *structure* of work groups in which social interaction took place. The character or type of work group is determined largely by technological requirements. In turn, the work group determines the kind of social relationship that is possible for its members.

Workers are placed along the main line and on sub-assembly operations according to the manpower requirements of the particular processes. In some places, as for example in sections of Body Trim, men are spaced along each side of the main conveyor. In other areas, as in a section of the Chassis Department, men are stationed at intervals under the line. Again, as in the interior body trim section, the men work inside the car itself.

For the most part, all of these men work in a specified area, completing their individual operations as the product moves down the line. These work areas, or so-called "stations," may overlap. That is to say, in performing his functions, a worker may move forward or back along the line into the general work areas of other workers.

Other assembly men, especially those on sub-assembly operations, work at benches or "bucks" in fixed positions. Some are grouped into teams, while others function quite independently of each other.

It was found that the social relationships of the workers could be divided into three broad categories determined by the technology of the line: (1) *isolated* workers performing functions independent of other workers; (2) workers performing functions independent of other workers, yet working in *close proximity* with one another; and (3) workers performing functions which are dependent upon a close *team* relationship.

To illustrate these categories, we turn to the diagrams which were drawn up by the interviewers with each worker. These diagrams show the placement of each man with reference to the line and the equipment. The pattern of social interaction is superimposed to show the number and location of men and the direction and frequency of their social interaction.

THE ISOLATED WORKER

A few men in the production departments of Plant X were socially isolated in the sense that they were stationed apart from other workers. Take for example the paint sprayer of wheels and small parts. This sprayer works alone and independently in a shed located at some distance from other paint operations. During the course of the working day he has little contact with others. His interaction rate, we would say, was zero. And he, like the few other isolates, indicated strongly that the lack of social interaction was important as one of his reasons for not liking the job.

WORKERS IN CLOSE PROXIMITY TO OTHERS BUT PERFORMING INDEPENDENT FUNCTIONS

Most assembly line workers, especially those on the main line, may be classified in this group. Take, for example, the polishers shown in the illustration section. One man polishes the trunk compartment lid, another the doors on the right side of the body,

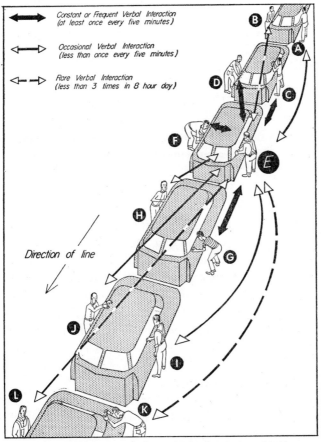

Fig. 3. Social Interaction Pattern of Typical Main Assembly Line Worker — Polisher, Paint Department.

another the doors on the left side, while a fourth worker polishes the right rear fender, and his opposite number the left rear fender. In so far as his own polishing operations are concerned, each worker is quite independent of the other workers in his section. Figure 3 shows the social relationship of a single worker, the door polisher on the left side of the line, to all those who work in his area.

As shown in Figure 3, cars are moved onto the main line by the trucker, A. Then C and D perform the first operation, polishing the trunk. Next E (the worker with whom we are directly concerned) and F polish the doors on either side. Next the fenders are polished by G and H, and finally the quarter panels are polished by I and J.

There are ten men in all whom E considers as members of his work group (A to J in Figure 3). His closest social contact, however, is with only four of these men. They include F, the polisher opposite him, C and D, whose operations immediately precede his, and G, who works next to him in the immediately succeeding polishing operation. The remaining men, A, B, H, I, and J, are part of E's larger group, but are not as close, either spatially or socially, as C, D, F, and G. In fact, E is not related to anyone in this "work group" other than by proximity. E can polish doors as they come to him, regardless of whether the men behind him have completed their polishing operations.

The above pattern is typical and basic for many, if not most, main line workers. The men from A to J comprise a group *only* from E's point of view. If we looked at the relationship pattern of G, his immediate group would be E, F, H, and I. It would not include C and D, who were clearly members of E's immediate group. Thus each man on the line has a slightly different group from that of the man next to him.

The polishers illustrate another feature of many assembly line work groups. Each worker is restricted because of fixed equipment to a limited range of movement along the line. He has a hand polishing machine which is suspended above him by wires. It cannot be moved at will to any location in the section, but runs along the overhead track only up to the point where the workers in adjacent groups begin their operations.

In some work groups there is considerably greater freedom of movement up and down the line, thus increasing the range of potential contacts a worker can have with others. In a sense this variation might be considered as constituting a separate type of relationship pattern. Using Figure 3 to illustrate, a man in a position similar to J, if he were not bound by fixed equipment, could move up several operations to the area of say B's position, greatly increasing the size of his social group.

Utility men on line operations are examples of even greater mobility. They fill in on the various jobs for a section of as many as thirty men. Similarly, in some sections the foreman allows men to alternate between different jobs from time to time. The significance of this free interaction for men who move over a broad area of the line, for utility men and for those allowed to shift jobs, comes out sharply — and favorably — in the interviews.

Another variation of the interaction pattern may be noted when a man on line operations can make contact not only with men right on his own line, as shown in our two previous examples, but with men on a completely different section of the line. The men in the other section may, for example, be working on a parallel line running close by, but in a different direction, as shown in Figure 4.

Notice here that B's immediate social group is not made up entirely of men working on similar operations. It comprises A and C, whose relationship to B is similar to the relationship of the polishers described earlier; but it also includes X, Y, and Z, who are on another section of the line at a later stage of assembly operations. Nevertheless, the same principle noted in the case of the polishers holds true here, namely that the group is not identifiable as separate and homogeneous for all the men in a given area, but rather shifts from one man to the next through the successive operations.

WORKERS PERFORMING FUNCTIONS WHICH ARE DEPENDENT
ON OTHERS IN A CLOSE TEAM RELATIONSHIP

A few operations, mainly in sub-assembly, require two or three or as many as fifteen men working directly with one another in a clearly defined group or team. The simplest type is found where two men coöperate with one another as partners. As an example, in a sub-assembly section of the Metal Department two men assist one another directly in spot welding operations on rear quarter panels. One man places two pieces of formed sheet

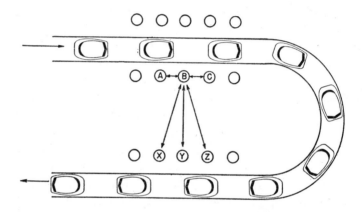

Fig. 4. Social Interaction Pattern, Main Assembly Line (Variation).

metal in a fixed position on a jig while his partner spot welds the pieces together. Both men are located at some distance from either the men who make up the metal stock in preceding operations or those working in the succeeding operation. Spatially they are separate from other workers, and in this instance the only "constant" or "frequent" interaction takes place between themselves.

Examples of partner teams may be found in some places along the main line itself. In the Trim Department two men must set the large pre-assembled instrument panels in place and attach certain parts of them to the panel support. They work together and right beside each other in the forward section of the body as it moves down the line. Simultaneously a pair of "headliners" may be working in the rear section of the body hanging cloth headlining material to the ceiling of the car. Both jobs require a close coördination of motions, and this interdependence of the partners requires and permits almost constant social interaction.

In other areas of the plant (usually in sub-assembly operations), it is possible to find larger team units. In the assembly of finished front fenders and grilles, five men work together as a unit on "bucks" or supports. Pre-assembled fenders are con-

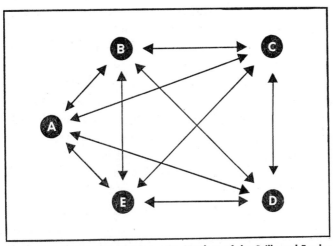

Fig. 5. Social Interaction Pattern among Members of the Grille and Fender Assembly Team. All members of the unit interact with all other members. The group remains the same for all five individuals.

veyed into the work area on overhead trolleys. Grilles move in on ground conveyors. The units are set on stationary bucks and bolted together, and then the entire assemblage is conveyed to the main line. (An illustration of this operation may be seen at page 21.) In the process of grille and fender assembly, workers are grouped around the stationary buck in close proximity with one another. Each man in the five-man team is functionally dependent upon the others. Each worker can and does interchange operations with the others. The pattern of interaction for such a group is shown in Figure 5.

This team is not only a functional and spatial unit. Each member can talk with every other member, and interaction is fairly equal and constant. Subjectively these men feel that they are an identifiable social, as well as work, group. Contrast this pattern with that of the polishers where no two men had the same group. The significance of this distinction in pattern of interaction is brought out below in the evaluations of the workers.

Reviewing the three broad types of relationship patterns — the isolated workers, the independent workers in proximity to others, and the dependent workers in teams — it was found that a large majority of men in our sample fell into the second category. On the main line there were fewer teams than in sub-assembly areas.

How were the above distinctions in group patterns related to job satisfaction? Unfortunately, a clear-cut answer is not possible, since many of the workers' subjective comments do not lend themselves to statistical summary. But some facts *are* clear. Isolated workers disliked their jobs and gave social isolation as the principal reason. As one of them said, "I miss talking. I'm alone in the paint shed and don't like it." *

A team worker was usually aware of the fact that he worked with others in an identifiable group. Most of them looked upon this fact favorably as shown by the following comments:

I'm in a team of six. One man works inside the car body right with me. We're good friends. So are the others in my group. We talk and kid all day long. Makes the job sort of fun. I'd much prefer working with others than alone.

I work off the line making bumper guards. I have a partner. The two of us work as a team. We talk all the time. A work's standards man told us we were the only two in the plant that worked as a team.

* The authors recognize that under certain conditions of hiring and employment selection, men might be found and assigned to such jobs because of their "aptitude" for working alone. This kind of selective hiring was not used at Plant X.

I work with another fellow. He pulls the fender back and I tighten it with bolts. If we do it wrong, it costs a lot of money. We have a lot of fun and talk all the time.

There are about a dozen hood fitters where I am. Everybody helps the other out. I work especially with one other. We coöperate together. I'm not a great talker, but it's nice to have somebody else around, kid around once in a while.

We talk freely. It's teamwork — that's what it adds up to.

I have one partner in a group of five fellows. We all help one another and change jobs for variety. No throat cutting. It's nice to work in that kind of atmosphere.

The majority of the men, as was pointed out before, do not work in groups which are recognizable as distinct teams. They spoke about being able to talk to others near them, but only rarely did they use expressions about "our team," "our own group," or "my partners." There was little of what the social psychologist would call "in-group awareness." One man on the line put it this way: "I've been here over a year, and I hardly know the first names of the men in the section where I work."

We did find some men, not in actual teams, who appeared to have a distinct awareness of being part of a group. These were men whose jobs were mobile. They could move around an entire section of operations and get to know and talk with all the men in the section; they were not anchored to one station. Utilitymen gave special emphasis to the advantages of moving around and talking with others. Here are several examples:

I can talk to any of the fifty-five different men as I walk around my section. I know everyone in the department by their first name.

My job takes me all around. I can talk to all the fellows at one time or another in our section.

I'm in a repair pit. I like it because I can do the work and talk with a lot of others. I don't stay in one place. That's why I get a chance to talk to the forty fellows in my section.

In general, it would appear that the social aspects of the job were important and that differences in group structure were reflected in attitudes.

The broader question remains: How important is social contact when compared with other aspects of the total job? Was the fact of social interaction with fellow workers on the job more important as a reason for liking the job than, say, working conditions or the advantages of the job in terms of good pay and security?

To answer this question, we turn to the rating scale of elements in which workers listed their principal reasons for liking or disliking the job. Among the fifty-two favorable and unfavorable job elements, two concerned what we have called "social interaction." One of these items in the favorable column was "can talk with others." On the dislike side, its counterpart was listed "cannot talk with others." * Only one man gave this social element as a primary reason for liking the present job, but nine men listed "can talk with others" as either second or third reason for liking the job. On the dislike side, only one man gave "cannot talk with others" as the primary reason for disliking the job.

Is the conclusion to be drawn that social interaction on the job was not important? In our judgment, no. The qualitative comments show that for many men the ability to talk and joke on the job was meaningful and important, even though they often expressed this evaluation negatively. For example, talking "relieves the tension," or "it makes the time go faster," and so forth. To be sure, none were so conscious of these advantages that they expressed them as principal reasons for liking the job. Rather, they took them for granted. When men were restricted, however, as the isolates were, they expressed themselves very strongly against their enforced denial of social contact. When

* There were actually two more items which were "social" in essence, but they are not included here, since they do not concern the immediate job situation. They were: "chance to meet people" and its opposite, "no chance to meet people."

they were grouped in identifiable teams or when there was mobility within the group, their reaction came out strongly and favorably in their qualitative comments. Or when workers began to compare what their jobs might be like *without* the opportunity for social interaction they were emphatic: "If you weren't talking . . . you'd go nuts," for example. It would seem plausible to conclude, then, that if the rules of the company were such, or the technological organization so constituted, as to eliminate group activity and social interaction, this fact would have provoked sharp opposition and stood high on the dislike side of the rating scale.

SUMMARY

(1) Slightly less than half of the workers had frequent social interaction with others near them. Slightly more than half had infrequent social interaction.

(2) Factors such as noise, pace, and character of the work often restricted men from talking as freely as they might otherwise have done. These limitations were consciously recognized by the workers as a source of frustration.

(3) The nature of the assembly process determined the functional relationships of workers and thus had a crucial bearing on their social groupings. The largest number of men, including most of those on the main conveyor line, were related to each other through proximity and not through interdependent function. Each man had a slightly different group from that of the man next to him. Few were conscious of being members of any identifiable social group.

(4) In a few cases men worked in almost complete isolation. Such workers gave social isolation as an important reason for not liking the job.

(5) In some areas, usually not on a moving line, men worked in teams. Geographically they were apart from other operations. Each man was functionally dependent upon his partner or his teammates, and social interaction was virtually constant. Jobs

were usually rotated within the group. According to the qualitative comments, most of these men were favorably aware of the fact that they constituted a work team.

(6) In certain instances, even on the moving conveyor, a group consciousness was found among those workers who were able to move into different operations in their section from time to time. This was true for utilitymen, some repairmen, and some workers whose foremen allowed them to rotate their jobs throughout a given section. Such workers named these features as desirable characteristics of their jobs.

(7) The ultimate value and importance of the more satisfying *kinds* of social relationships were demonstrated by the qualitative comments. In discussing the amount of talking they did, the isolates were the most vehemently negative. The largest group, those working side by side but independently, were more likely to refer to their social relations in the negative terms of how they would feel were they not able to talk, and of the effects of interaction in counteracting other job tensions. In marked contrast, those who were members of true teams spoke of their group interaction in positive and cheerful terms.

6 PAY AND SECURITY

How important were economic factors in the total job picture of assembly workers at Plant X? This is the question this chapter will try to answer. In preliminary interviewing we discovered that many of the workers had been attracted to Plant X by its reputation for "high pay." As one worker commented, "My friends all think I made a good move. It's a large firm, working almost steadily. The pay is better and steadier than most places."

"Why did you decide to apply for a job at Plant X?" was asked toward the beginning of every interview. The results are shown in Table 8. Note that fifty said they had applied for jobs at Plant X because their jobs were about to be or had been terminated. This disappearance of jobs had occurred because of reductions in force, shutdowns, or company failures. Twenty-nine said their old jobs were not steady enough to assure them an adequate income. Over three-quarters of the workers interviewed had been motivated in turning to Plant X for employment mainly by economic factors.

That economics operated strongly in bringing workers to Plant X was confirmed by our rating scale of "likes" and "dislikes" on the old and the new jobs. "Poor pay" and "work not steady" were listed as first reasons for disliking previous jobs more often than for all the remaining twenty-four reasons combined.

The workers freely expressed their feelings and opinions upon the economic factors of both their Plant X jobs and their previous ones. Before analyzing these responses, we will turn to the actual facts about wages and methods of payment at Plant X.

The economic attraction which Plant X exercised upon the manufacturing area in which it is located is easy to explain. Wages were lower in this area than for comparable occupations in many, though not all, other parts of the country. Wages for the automobile industry are 20 to 25 per cent higher than the average for manufacturing as a whole.* In view of the promise

TABLE **8**

Reasons Given for Applying for Job at Plant X

Reason	Number of Men
Last job unsatisfactory (pay)	59
Last job terminated (or about to be)	50
Last job unsatisfactory (unsteady work)	29
General interest in automobile work	19
Last job unsatisfactory (working conditions)	7
Last job unsatisfactory (distance from work)	5
No opportunity for advancement	4
Last job unsatisfactory (poor hours)	3
Other reasons	4
Total	180

of high wages at Plant X which came at a time following postwar cutbacks in production in the area, it was perhaps not surprising that there were ten times as many applications for work as there were jobs available.

The actual differential between wages on previous jobs and wages at Plant X was as follows. Median hourly wages for workers' jobs prior to being employed at Plant X were $1.05 per hour, or $42.00 per week, not including overtime earnings. Median hourly wages for the assembly plant workers were $1.51, or over $60.40 per week, not including overtime.**

* *Monthly Labor Review*, vol. 69, no. 6 (December, 1949), Table C-1, p. 711, shows average gross weekly earnings of production workers or non-supervisory employees for all "manufacturing" in June, 1949, were $54.51, and for "automobiles" $66.94.

** These figures are as of June, 1949. The spread would be reduced somewhat if one considered that former jobs may also have been adjusted

Figure 6 shows in detail the contrast between previous earnings and those on present Plant X jobs. Notice the wide spread of

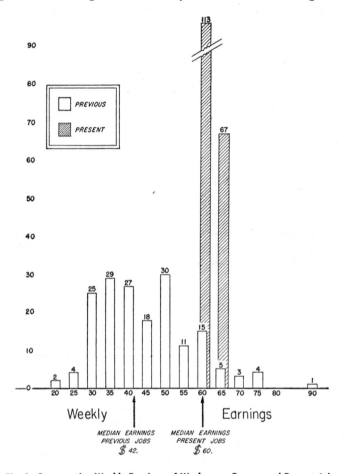

Fig. 6. Comparative Weekly Earnings of Workers on Former and Present Jobs.

weekly wages on previous jobs, ranging from a low of $20 (nearly the statutory minimum) to a high of over $75 for a few, but centering in the low "forties." Thus a small number of workers

upward during the period between quitting previous jobs and the above date. It is questionable, however, whether the adjustment would have amounted to more than 15 cents an hour or $6.00 per week.

accepted less money when going to work at Plant X, but the overwhelming majority experienced a substantial increase.

A significant fact about Plant X jobs is the relatively narrow spread of wages. All of our sample fell either in the $60 or the $65 per week average group. Table 9 gives the actual breakdown of pay for the 180 men in terms of assembly plant wages for a straight forty-hour week schedule. Except for the single worker listed in the last line of Table 9, the wage differential from the lowest to the highest was only $3.60 per week, with the largest number of workers (ninety-five) all receiving the same rate of $60.40.*

TABLE **9**

Base Pay (Weekly) for Typical Production Workers at Plant X [a]
(*Based on Hourly Rate x 40*)

Base Pay (Per Week)	Number of Men
$60.40	95
61.20	16
62.00	2
62.40	20
63.20	5
64.00	41
66.00	1

[a] Sample of 180 production workers.

This narrow wage range (between lowest and highest job classes) is a characteristic of almost all mass production industries and particularly of the automotive industry. The introduction of conveyors and machine hand tools has narrowed the wage distance between the day laborer's job and that of the skilled craftsman. Many mass production jobs, certainly jobs such as those found in automotive assembly operations, require greater skill than that of the ordinary "unskilled" worker. On the other hand, individual work operations have been either

* There was a small number of specialists in the production departments who earned over $1.65 per hour ($66.00 per week), but since there were so few and their jobs were not typical, they were not included in the sample.

so mechanized or so fractionalized (broken down into simple tasks) that, as we remarked earlier, craft skills have been virtually eliminated. One result of this technological development has been wage standardization.

Another cause of wage standardization has been union policy. Throughout the history of collective bargaining in the mass production industries, and especially in the automobile industry, unions have pushed in the direction of further wage uniformity on production jobs. Pay increases for higher-paying jobs have been generally sacrificed in order to raise the standards for traditionally low-wage jobs.

The importance of wage uniformity for our present inquiry will be discussed in Chapter IX in connection with the problems of advancement among the men at Plant X. The point is made here primarily to show the sharp contrast in wage rates and wage structure between the jobs which the men formerly held and those they took when they came to the assembly line. The contrast helps to explain why most workers, although disliking certain features of assembly line work, had no intention of seeking employment elsewhere.

Another aspect of the wage picture should be mentioned. There were large numbers of men, especially those formerly in manufacturing, who had been paid piece rates or had received pay on the basis of individual or group incentive systems. At Plant X all production workers received straight hourly wages. This method of wage payment is typical of the industry, and understandably so. The conveyor, rather than the individual worker, determines the pace of work. Because of this conveyor system, a worker who finishes his own operations cannot speed up the number of units which move through his particular station; nor can he increase the total number of units to be produced per hour. He can, of course, temporarily decrease his own work speed by not completing all the units brought to him by the conveyor, and in so doing will eventually force a slow down of the entire line. Even those workers on off-line jobs who "build up a bank" (that is, build for stock) can only vary their work rate within narrow limits, since their pace, too, is geared closely to the speed of the main line.

Under such circumstances, it is obvious why an individual piece work system, or even a group "bonus" system of payment, has not been considered feasible. Some workers liked this fact, others did not, their preferences stemming from previous job experience. Some were severely critical of the incentive plans which had been associated with their previous jobs, stating that they "had to work like hell" to make a living wage. Others, especially skilled craftsmen, looked back with nostalgia on their old jobs because the piece work system had allowed them to make even more than their present hourly wages on the assembly line. A third group of workers indicated that they had liked their former jobs because a piece work system made it possible for a man to determine when and for how long he could take a rest period.

A further significant difference from previous jobs which involved a third of the workers interviewed, was the feature of "steady work" and hence steady income from Plant X employment. An analysis of the dominant industries in this area shows why previous work was unsteady. In two of the major industries, work was either seasonal or cyclical. Plants operated for months on a peak load basis, then slumped to low production and sometimes to no production at all for extended periods of time.

It will be recalled that the automobile industry itself was once plagued by periods of shutdowns, principally for two reasons. Inventory systems had not been perfected to allow for continued year round production, so that plants sometimes shut down for as long as three months while inventory was being taken. Naturally, inventories are still taken, but the shutdown has been considerably shortened. Second, the system of yearly model changes made for serious problems of retooling and scheduling. As during inventory, assembly plants either closed or drastically reduced operations in model change periods. These periods now have been eliminated.

To the workers these facts simply meant no pay during the shutdown. Fortunately for the men at Plant X, these conditions have largely been eliminated. They looked upon their jobs in terms of a steady and comparatively high income.

We now turn to the actual comments of Plant X workers on the "economic" aspects of their jobs. Later we shall evaluate their importance in comparison with other elements in the total job situation. The question was asked: "If you had a chance to take a job outside Plant X, what would you do?" A large majority of workers said that, although they would like to have another *kind* of job, it would have to provide as much pay and security as the ones they were holding at Plant X. Here are typical comments:

I'd take any job that would pay the same amount of money. The work is too hard. But the money would have to be about as good before I'd leave. Eventually I'd like to get into drafting. I've had some training in it.

I'd prefer a job off assembly line work. I'd take any job off assembly line work if I could get equal pay, but I wouldn't leave Company X unless I got almost as much pay.

If I had to make the choice of quitting the masonry contracting business and starting at the plant all over again, I'd still go to the plant. It's more steady and less seasonal than my old job. Also better working hours.

I wouldn't take a job outside. Where else can you get $60 a week? Maybe in ——— I could, but the work isn't steady. Isn't that right? Why, God, yes, of course it's right.

I'd stay. It's a big company and they are not a fly-by-night outfit. The job means security. I liked the job in the ——— factory and I made more money, but the ——— business was always up and down.

Another group of men, approximately one-fourth of the total, indicated clearly that they would be willing to take a wage cut if they could find another job *not* in an assembly plant. A majority of this group expressed themselves favorably on pay, general working conditions, and supervision. It was the immediate job —

its pace, repetitiveness, and so forth — which made them willing to take another job at less money. Here is a typical remark:

I'd leave and take another job at $50 a week. I'd take almost any job to get away from there. A body can't stand it there. My health counts most. What's the use of money if you ruin your health?

On the other hand, many workers, especially those not on line jobs, said that they did not want to leave Plant X.

I intend to stay. My job is better than a lot of them. It must be better when I hear how awful the guys on the line say it is. They say they're dead in the morning. That's why I'd rather work where I do [spot-welding in sub-assembly] and not on the line. Also I'm making as good money as I could make anywhere else.

I'd stay. A guy will get somewhere here. It's a good place for advancement.

A job outside would have to be as steady and pay a hell of a lot more. I wouldn't take a cut to leave. The job I have now is O. K.

We noticed with interest that a great many of the workers at some point in the interview spoke about getting out "and starting up my own little business." This kind of remark came out most frequently when they were asked the qusetion, "If you had a chance to take a job outside . . ." The sentiment of a sprayer in the Trim Department was repeated many times.

If I could be my own boss, or work myself up to that position, I'd leave. Otherwise, I might as well stay where I am.

A remark reflecting a purely economic motivation for keeping the present job was rare. Here is one of this type:

Any job that paid more I'd take. I'm out for the money and that's all . . . And this place isn't exactly a rest home, you know.

Through another question, still further information was drawn out regarding the economic factors of the job. Workers were asked: "What does your wife think of your job at Plant X?" Most of the favorable answers centered on the factors of good pay and steady income. Only a small minority of the men failed to mention one or the other. Here are some of the more typical answers:

She's glad I have a good-paying job and steady.

She likes the money and security. It enabled us to get married.

Wife: I wanted him to go to Plant X even before he applied. It's a wonderful thing to be able to plan on a certain amount of money.

She's quite mercenary; money is the main thing.

Wife: The job was hard on him until he got used to it.

She likes it all right — PAY!

During the interviews, we were struck by the strong sense of planning for the future. Many families for the first time were looking forward with some confidence to buying their homes. Others pointed with pride to new furniture, kitchen equipment, or a television set. "We would never have had these things if it weren't for my husband's good steady job at Plant X."

We noted in many instances that the friends and neighbors of workers looked favorably upon the wage aspects of Plant X jobs. Because most men were making higher wages than their friends and neighbors, many thought that their community placed them in a higher social status or envied their economic position. Even so, most men hastened to point out that friends and neighbors were fully aware of the disadvantages of the work.

Such comments and many others like them pointed up the fact that good pay and steady income were important elements in the total job picture. What was the relation of this economic element to the other job elements already discussed?

Among the twenty-six elements of job likes and dislikes used on the "total job" check list were included good pay (or poor pay), steady work (or work not steady), and benefits. Taken together, we have labeled these the economic factors of the total job. Of the 180 workers interviewed, there were 126 who gave good pay as the primary reason for liking their Plant X jobs. Another twenty-one placed steady work first in importance. On the dislike side of the check list, only one worker mentioned poor pay as the main unfavorable feature of his present job; only one said "work not steady." Interestingly enough, no one raised the question of "no benefits" as a reason for not liking the job.*

In other words, 147 men, or slightly more than 80 per cent of our sample, considered economic factors as the principal reason for liking their present jobs. This high percentage naturally subordinated the other job categories: general working conditions, supervision, the immediate job, and others. Still more striking is the almost complete absence of checks in the dislike columns of the rating scale. Even when asked for second or third reasons for disliking the present job, the workers made no criticism of economic factors.

Turning to ratings on the workers' previous jobs, there was a marked contrast in response. Fifty-four, or less than a third of the sample, considered the good economic features of the previous jobs as first in importance for liking these jobs. Eighty-one men gave poor pay or work not steady as the principal reason for disliking their former jobs. This substantiates the qualitative remarks referred to earlier regarding reasons why workers took jobs at Plant X.

Because of the large number (147 out of 180) of favorable responses regarding the economic factors of the present job, we were curious to find out more precisely how important the single element — pay — was in the total job picture. Of the 147, there were twenty-one who listed steady work as the principal reason for liking their present jobs. Of the remaining 126 (those who checked good pay), we asked the question, "Is the pay the only reason why you are keeping your job at Plant X?" Eighty men responded in the affirmative.

---

* Even the pressing question of pensions, which highlighted the steel dispute going on at the time of our study, did not appear important to these men at the time. Considering the fact that the average age of Plant X workers was twenty-seven, this is not too surprising.

SUMMARY

(1) Over three-quarters of the workers had been mainly motivated in turning to Plant X for employment by economic factors.

(2) The differential between previous and present wages for the workers interviewed was substantial, $1.05 per hour as compared with $1.51, $42.00 per week as compared with $60.40.

(3) On previous jobs there was a spread of $50.00 between the lowest and highest weekly wages; on present Plant X jobs, a spread of only $3.60.

(4) Chiefly accounting for this narrow difference were technological factors and union policy.

(5) Steady and secure employment at Plant X contrasted for many workers with seasonal work by financially unstable firms and with unemployment. These facts were reflected in the qualitative comments of workers, of their wives, and of their neighbors.

(6) Eighty per cent of the sample considered the economic factors as the principal reason for liking their present jobs; fifty-four, or less than a third of the number, considered the economic features of their previous jobs first in importance. Eighty-one gave poor pay or work not steady as the prime reason for disliking their previous jobs.

7 THE WORKER AND SUPERVISION

The importance of the worker-foreman relationship in in-plant society can hardly be questioned. Through the foreman the worker daily meets management face to face. From him he receives most of the company's directives and orders which affect him, and through the foreman he is told to communicate his own requests or complaints to upper management.

The presence of a union representative in the plant may challenge or divide the authority which foremen of an earlier day exercised. It may also alter the character of the foreman-worker relationship, but it can hardly be said to lessen its importance either for efficiency or job satisfaction. Upon these and other themes, a substantial body of sociological literature has now grown up. In fact, it may be that the new emphasis on this relationship has caused some devaluation of other important elements in the total job situation. In any case, the area of relations between the foreman and the worker unquestionably is one basic factor in that situation and an important determinant of satisfaction or dissatisfaction on the job.

Turning to Plant X, we find the supervisory structure typical of most automobile assembly plants. Each production department has four levels: Superintendent, Assistant Superintendent, General Foreman, and Foreman. Above each production department are two levels: Production Manager and Plant Manager. In other words, there are six managerial levels above the worker, or three levels between the worker and top departmental supervision.

We shall touch briefly on the relationships of workers to upper supervision and management, which for the most part are infrequent and indirect, and deal more intensively with foreman-worker relationships, which are direct and personal.*

In studying all these relationships, we began by recording the actual amount and direction of contact between a man and supervision starting with his foreman. The men were asked: "In an average day, how often does the foreman talk with you? Often (at least once an hour), occasionally (at least twice a day), or rarely (once a day or less)?"

Sixty workers in our sample of 180 reported that the foreman talked with them at least once an hour; eighty-three that he talked with them at least twice a day; and thirty-seven that he talked with them once a day or less.

Qualitative comments by the men about their foremen (as will be shown later) suggested a relatively informal and friendly relationship on the part of the majority. There also appeared to be an adequate two-way relationship. One structural fact which helped to make this type of relationship possible was the relatively small number of men per foreman. This number ranged from fifteen to twenty-five men.

It has been the experience of one of the authors that foremen on some automobile assembly lines initiate most contacts with workers, and mainly for the purpose of exhorting them to keep up with the line. At Plant X this condition was not found.

The men were also asked to indicate contacts with supervision in their departments above the rank of foreman. Fifty-five reported that they talked with their general foreman once a week or less; fifteen said one to three times a month; and eighty-eight reported less than once a month. (Twenty-two reported that they were not sure who was their general foreman.) Thus nearly half of those interviewed said they had interaction with their general foreman less than once a month.

---

* Contact between production workers and the staff departments was so slight that discussion of this point has been omitted here. Worker contacts with the Personnel and Inspection Departments were occasionally reflected in worker interviews.

The rarity of contact with top departmental supervision was naturally more pronounced. Seventy per cent of the workers reported having contact with their superintendents less than once a month. Contact with the "front office," either the production manager or the plant manager, was even less frequent.

Both the quantity and quality of social interaction in a plant appear to be determined mainly by three factors: (1) by the size of the unit within which interaction takes place, (2) by requirements or limitations of the process, and (3) by management policy and custom. In small plants, especially those plants with a work force under five hundred, interaction with all ranks of supervision, including top management, obviously occurs far more frequently. This fact has long been recognized by both industrial sociologists and employers. Less attention has been paid to the effects of technological factors and company policy on in-plant social interaction.

In order to contrast the interaction pattern of workers and supervision at Plant X with another kind of industrial unit, a comparison was made with a department in a steel fabricating mill studied by the authors. The results are shown in Figure 7.

In both instances, interaction between worker and foreman was frequent, but in the steel fabricating mill, interaction between worker and upper supervision was far more frequent. In the steel mill the nature of the process, the physical layout of operations, and the high degree of worker skills made for a closer relationship between the men and upper supervision. Supervisors above the foreman level often consulted with individual men, especially the key workers, on production problems, since the judgment of the individual worker was important. On the automobile assembly line, however, because of the high degree of mechanization and fractional assembly, there appeared to be less reason or need for upper supervision to discuss production matters with individual workers.   •

So much for a brief account of interaction between workers and supervision at Plant X. We turn now to workers' attitudes

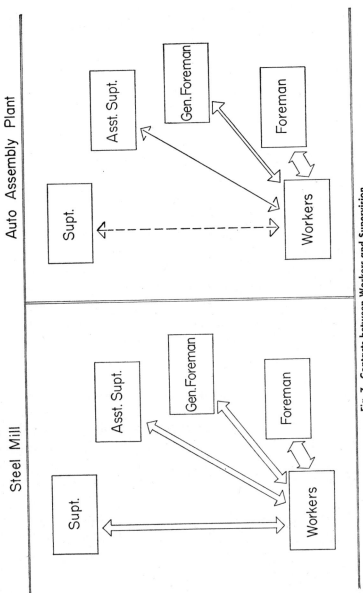

Fig. 7. Contacts between Workers and Supervision.

toward and opinions about their immediate job supervisors and the relative importance of a good or a bad foreman in the total job situation.

A large majority of the workers interviewed thought the foremen "got on well with the men at Plant X" and told why. Only fifteen men out of the 180 gave "poor bosses" as either their first, second, or third reason for disliking their jobs at Plant X. In other words, the workers in this plant rated immediate job supervisors high.*

Experience in interviewing workers over a period of several years had taught the authors that many men hesitate to give a direct evaluation of their immediate supervisors. Accordingly, the interviewer and the worker discussed supervision in general, and then the question was asked: "How well would you say your foreman gets along with the men?"

Of the 178 workers who gave some kind of answer, sixty-eight (38.2 per cent) said that the foreman got along very well with the men. Another sixty-one (34.3 per cent) answered that they got along fairly well. Eleven (6.2 per cent) held neutral or mixed attitudes. Eighteen (10.1 per cent) answered "not so well," and the remaining twenty (11.2 per cent) said "very poorly."

Thus almost three-quarters of all the workers said that their foremen got along very well or fairly well with their men. When asked whether their answers were reasons for liking or not liking the job, the results were as follows: 124 of the 129 who had answered "very" or "fairly well" said that their foremen constituted one reason why they liked their jobs. Of the thirty-eight who answered "not so well" or "very poorly," twenty-eight said this was one reason for not liking their jobs. In effect, the workers stated that a good foreman (or at least one who got along with the men) was an element in the degree of job satisfaction. They were not,

---

* During the early period of operations, there was some hint that foremen brought in from another plant were resented as outsiders. However, by the time this study was made the resentment had all but disappeared. The local plant was then promoting many local men to foremen's jobs.

however, saying *how* important comparatively the foreman factor was.

Another possible indication of how the workers evaluated the job of foreman is the fact that at least one in every five some day hoped to become a foreman himself.

In addition to this specific question, we analyzed *all* the qualitative references to foremen recorded in the interviews. Wherever a worker spoke favorably or unfavorably about his foreman, he almost always explained why he thought or felt as he did. Of all the comments recorded, 244 qualitative remarks could be distinguished. Of these, 174 were favorable and seventy were unfavorable.

Among the favorable comments, it was found that thirty-one men said nothing other than to indicate that their foremen got on with the men very or fairly well. The remaining 143 favorable comments fall into four groups. One is made up of brief remarks, usually in the form of adjectival phrases. These include "nice guy, good guy, damn good, O.K., regular fellow, good scout, good personality, well liked," and others. All in all, there were fifty-one expressions of opinion by workers in these eight terms or in terms almost identical to them.

In another category are those comments in which the attitude was expressed in negative but favorable terms. That is to say, the foreman was liked because he did not do things which the men disliked. Such comments included "doesn't bother us, doesn't bawl the men out, doesn't talk too much, leaves you alone," and a few others like them. All together there were twenty-three comments of this nature.

The third category includes remarks of a positive character. They revealed desirable social traits such as "tries to be fair and square, gets along with the men, tries to help out, tries to show you, jokes with the men, listens to reason, willing to talk to you, appreciates good work." There were forty-seven comments of this nature.

A fourth group comprised remarks indicating respect for the

foreman's character or competence because "he works hard, knows his job, is on hand when needed." The ways in which the men expressed favorable attitudes toward their foremen may be seen in the following quotations:

He gets along with everybody. He works like a madman; right on the line with us.

A good foreman makes it one hundred per cent easier.

He's around all the time. We're lucky. He's a real good guy. If he got into trouble, the whole department would back him right up.

He's a pretty good foreman. Four or five out of this section don't like him, but somebody out of that many people won't like a foreman. He tries to coöperate with the union and the men, but still he's a company man.

We have a lot of shop talk together. It might be about the job, the men, or baseball. We talk on and off all day. Sometimes we yell at each other, but it doesn't mean anything.

He gets along good with just about all of the fellows. He gives you half a break.

My foreman is very coöperative. Always tells you what to do, but you can talk and ask him questions. Doesn't figure you're just a working man. You're partners with him.

I like him O. K. He comes from around here. The first boss came from another plant. After all, the foreman has to be a pusher and nobody likes to be pushed. He's got to hold his job. If he doesn't push, somebody else will get his job.

Turning to the unfavorable attitudes toward foremen expressed by the men, it will be recalled that only thirty-eight, or hardly one-fifth of the entire sample, thought that the foreman "didn't get along so well" or "got along very poorly with the men." Often these remarks were simply the opposites of those just recorded. Thus, we find statements such as "bosses the men too much, is a pusher, a driver, too much for production, stands over us, won't listen, treats the men like machines," and others. Some of the men described undesirable personality traits in such words as "excitable, sneaky, rude, stubborn." Some said simply that a fore-man "was not qualified to handle the men."

He's all right in some ways, but all the fellows say he won't ever listen to suggestions. His answers hurt you; he should use some psychology.

The men have no respect for the foreman. He's not suited for the job. This fellow is young and doesn't know anything about the job or getting work out of the men. Other bosses drive him. In his crude way, he can't get anything out of the men.

On our line everybody hates the foreman — his personality. He's an egotist. The job's gone to his head.

Some statements made by the men ascribed the undesirable behavior of a foreman not to the foreman himself but to his superiors. Of these there were seventeen comments, including such remarks as "he's on a spot, afraid of losing his job, too much pressure on him, a company man, doesn't have the authority." It may be said that the workers who disliked assembly line work rarely projected their feelings into dislike of their foremen. This appears to us an important finding. Even when a foreman appeared to be reinforcing disliked characteristics of the line — its pace, repetitiveness, or fatigue, for example — the worker tended to exonerate him by implying that such factors were beyond his personal control.

How did the average worker rate the factor of immediate supervisors within the total job picture at Plant X? We turn to the rating scale with its comparative weighting of job elements for light on this final question. The scale shows that although a majority of the men indicated that they had good foremen, only twenty-five men rated this factor among the first, second, or third reasons for liking their jobs at Plant X. Only six in the entire 180 mentioned it as the prime reason, while six named it as second, and thirteen as third. On the dislike side, only four men said that "poor bosses" was the principal reason for not liking the job, and seven gave it as second, four as the third reason. The factor of supervision was clearly crowded out both on the positive and on the negative side by more striking factors in the job situation. On the positive side, good pay and steady work were ahead (with 126 putting good pay and twenty-one putting steady work as the number one reason). On the negative side, elements connected with the immediate job (pacing, fatigue, and so forth) were more strongly disliked than "poor bosses." Undoubtedly if there had been a sudden drop in the character and competence of supervision, or if the number of men per foreman had been increased, this fact would have been reflected in the rising vote in the dislike column against "poor bosses" and a diminishing vote for some other undesirable factor.

SUMMARY OF WORKER-SUPERVISOR RELATIONSHIP AT PLANT X

(1) The supervisory structure in the production departments at Plant X reveals six supervisory levels, including the plant manager. Interaction was frequent between a majority of the workers and the first level of supervision, the foremen. With supervisors above the rank of foreman, it was infrequent.

(2) The technology of assembly line production did not interfere with a "healthy" two-way relationship between a man and his immediate supervisor. It appeared, however, to limit interaction between men and higher levels of supervision.

(3) Seventy-five per cent of the workers interviewed said their foremen got along very or fairly well with the men.

(4) Out of 244 qualitative remarks made about foremen, 174 were favorable and seventy were unfavorable.

(5) Features of assembly line work which were disliked by workers did not enter into their judgment of their foremen. A majority of the assembly line workers who reported unfavorably on such features reported favorably about their foremen.

(6) The workers considered the matter of a "good" or a "bad" foreman to be important, but as a factor in the total job satisfac-

tion, it was crowded out, both positively and negatively, by more striking factors: on the positive side by pay and steady work; on the negative side by unfavorable factors connected with the immediate job.

8 GENERAL WORKING CONDITIONS

The element in the total job situation of the American worker which perhaps has improved more rapidly than any other in recent years is "working conditions." As companies build new plants, they have been taking advantage of modern thinking in factory design, layout, lighting, safety, and health facilities. Plant X is no exception. In this chapter we try to rate the impact of such factors on job satisfaction. In so doing, we broaden somewhat the meaning of the term, "working conditions," to include not only the above features but also, for the sake of economy of discussion, hours and a few miscellaneous items such as distance from work. All of these we are considering as *one factor*, "general working conditions," in the total job situation. Here is the list of items:

(1) Working hours
(2) Working conditions
    (a) Temperature
    (b) Cleanliness
    (c) Safety
    (d) Ventilation
    (e) Noise
    (f) Hospital facilities
    (g) Cafeteria
    (h) Lighting
    (i) Other
(3) Miscellaneous items

As to working hours, Plant X operated on one eight-hour shift five days a week. The shift began at 7:30 A.M. and ended at 4:12

P.M., with forty-two minutes out for lunch. In addition to the regular schedule, a number of men worked overtime, especially during model changes. Some of these men spoke favorably of overtime because of the added pay; others were critical of it because the amount or occasion of overtime was unpredictable. On previous jobs many of the men had worked on night shifts or at other odd hours. They preferred the regular hours and the daylight shift which prevailed at Plant X.

Turning now to working conditions proper, Plant X was well-equipped with all modern facilities and installations, and they made a strong impression, especially during the first weeks of employment. Most workers had come to the plant from old factories with buildings fifty years old or more. Workers frequently pointed up these differences between previous and present jobs, together with the fact that few of them had ever worked in an automobile plant.

How, then, did the workers as a group react to general working conditions on their present jobs? Sixty per cent of the opinions were generally favorable. Thirty-one per cent were "mixed" or neutral. Nine per cent were generally unfavorable.

Clearly, a large majority considered that on the whole conditions were favorable. Workers were encouraged to discuss the specific items comprising general working conditions. The following remarks are typical:

I get better treatment at the plant hospital than in any place I've been. I never saw a hospital so well equipped.

They're right on the ball on safety conditions.

I like the cafeteria — it's clean.

The hours are very good.

You know you'll work eight straight daylight hours and be finished.

The ventilation is much better than it was on my last job.

Where I work the lighting is O.K.

They keep the place very clean.

While approving of conditions in general, occasionally workers picked out certain individual features as unfavorable.

The cafeteria is too far away. Poor food and high prices.

In my particular area the lighting is bad. Too many shadows.

The temperature in the winter is good, but it gets awfully hot in the summer.

We now turn to the question of the comparative rating of general working conditions factors with each other and with other elements in the total job situation. Eighty-eight men gave at least one of these factors as a first, second, or third main reason for liking their present jobs, but only eleven of the eighty-eight named any of the factors as the first reason for liking their assembly-line jobs. Analysis of the responses shows that the highest number of votes went to good hours, nearness to work, and working conditions, in that order.

On the dislike side of their present jobs, seventy-three men named at least one of the general working condition factors as a first, second, or third reason for disliking their present jobs. Eleven scored "poor working hours," eighteen mentioned "distance from work," and twelve disliked the fact that they were not on outdoor jobs.

Thirty-two mentioned some single factor associated with the surrounding conditions of particular jobs. In certain Paint Department operations workers complained of the heat. Some working inside cars complained of poor lighting. On spot welding jobs in the Metal Department noise was a source of irritation. These reactions of workers clearly concerned very specific features and were connected with particular jobs. On this point it will be recalled that only 9 per cent of all workers stated that working conditions *on the whole* were unfavorable.

How did workers rate general working conditions in relation to other job elements? A quantitative rating derived from the rating scale shows clearly that on the like side workers rated economic factors far higher than general working conditions. It shows that on the dislike side immediate job content was more important.

No precise quantitative comparison is possible between general working conditions and other factors in the total job situation such as supervision, relations with other workers, promotion and transfer, and the union, Nonetheless, qualitative comments make it clear that for many good working conditions did not compensate for disliked features of the job.

The lighting is O.K. There is some dust and fumes. The hospital and cafeteria are fine, but the work is an awful grind. People like us who never have worked on a line aren't used to the grind. Good working conditions don't help.

They [working conditions] don't make much difference to me. No time to notice these things anyway. You're too busy.

As jobs go, it's clean. Lighting is good. They keep the place pretty cool in summer and the electric fan blows warm air in the winter. All these other things are good, but they don't make the job good.

It's a new plant, so these things are O.K., but "conditions" don't make much difference one way or another.

The job is the most important thing, but surroundings help. At least they are much better than my last job.

These comments bear out the simple statements of comparative importance of general working conditions given earlier. The same theme runs through these and almost all of the qualitative remarks, namely, that good working conditions, however desirable, "don't make the job good," as so many workers bluntly put it. This finding is not new. But it does tend to contradict a popular notion held by some managers to the effect that good lighting, ventilation, cafeterias, and so forth, are the *most* important factors in bringing about job satisfaction.

Good working conditions are of course important in themselves, and it is probable that had conditions at Plant X been poor with regard to these factors, they would have had a marked effect in producing job dissatisfactions. We do know that workers who had had previous factory experience made sharp distinctions between former and present working conditions and stated further that at Plant X the situation had greatly changed for the better.

An attempt was made to relate the response to questions on general working conditions with the age, education, job classification, and so forth, of the individual workers. No correlations were found. On the broad question, "Would you say your job was very interesting, fairly interesting, not too interesting, or not at all interesting?" there appeared no marked differences between those workers who considered their general working conditions favorable and those who considered them unfavorable.

SUMMARY

(1) Plant X was a new unit with modern facilities for lighting, ventilation, cafeteria, and hospital. It operated on an eight-hour daylight schedule. For almost all of the workers such general working conditions were a marked improvement over conditions at their previous places of employment.

(2) Combining the list of elements making up general working conditions, it was found that a majority of the men at Plant X expressed generally favorable opinions, especially regarding hours of work and the physical facilities of the plant.

(3) When evaluating the importance of general working condition factors in comparison with other factors of the total job, pay and steady work were more important among the *liked* features of the job, and factors relating to the immediate job were of more importance as the features disliked about the job. In qualitative comments workers tended to minimize the effects of good working conditions as a factor in job satisfaction.

9 PROMOTION AND TRANSFER

Interest in promotion or transfer differs enormously not only among individuals of differing personalities but, according to the experience of the authors, among companies. At Plant X, the interest and preoccupation of workers in being either promoted or transferred from their present jobs to others was substantial.

Plant X was new. In order to begin operations with maximum efficiency, the corporation staffed the new organization with technicians and supervisory personnel from other operating plants. Available promotional openings were limited principally to nonsupervisory jobs.*

Other factors affected the system of promotions and transfers. These were (1) company policy, (2) the structure of job classes, and (3) the seniority system determined by the labor agreement.

Consider the first factor, company policy. During the early period of operations it was necessary to train large numbers of workers to perform given tasks adequately. Therefore, newly hired workers were informed that they were being employed for a specific job and that they should not expect to move around on different jobs or to be promoted quickly to higher paying or supervisory positions. The company reasoned that production might be impaired if such changes were encouraged in the new plant.

Since the general policy was to "promote from within" rather than to hire from outside, management expected that as time went on, normal turnover in hourly wage jobs and supervisory

---

* In spite of this, twenty-six men were promoted to temporary or permanent foreman positions within the first two years of operation.

positions would allow for more upward mobility. Also, workers who had once learned their jobs would be in a better position to take over other jobs in temporary and permanent transfers.

The second factor tending to limit job mobility is the job classification structure in assembly plant work. A characteristic of jobs on assembly lines is their limited range of skills. Almost every job has been broken down into a relatively simple set of motions, so that there is little gradation in skills between a job in one section of the line and one in another section. Translated in terms of wages, there is little spread between the lowest and highest job classes. The wage range of our group, for example, was hardly more than twelve cents an hour. Two-thirds of the workers in the two largest departments received exactly the same wage. Thus, for most workers there was little *financial* incentive for promotion among production jobs.* Except for a few jobs, distinct steps in a promotional ladder were lacking. This fact contrasts somewhat sharply with other industries in which jobs are not as closely tied to mass production principles.

There is a third factor which enters the picture of job mobility in the automobile industry. According to the contract with the union, promotions are dependent upon ability, merit, capacity, and seniority. In actual practice, seniority is often of great importance, so that only those men with highest seniority in a given job class may normally expect a promotion. According to the contract, transfers are not subject to seniority limitations, nor are men limited to transfers within a given department. But here again seniority is given consideration, and in actual practice the tendency is to discourage transfers from one department to another.

These three factors operating against job mobility — certain features of company policy, the structure of job classifications, and the seniority system — constitute a generalized statement of

---

* In a recent study of a steel fabricating plant, the base rate wage range of an average production department ran from $1.25 to $1.89 an hour, covering more than eighteen job classifications.

a condition. The degree to which this condition actually influenced Plant X in restricting transfers or promotions could only be determined by a study of the record over an extended period.

In any case, the workers themselves appeared relatively optimistic over their chances for advancement at Plant X, at least as compared with their chances on the jobs they had left. This may have been due in part to the fact that the men were aware that the plant was new. Two-thirds of the men said there was little opportunity for promotion on their previous jobs. Less than half considered this true of their assembly line jobs.* From the worker's point of view, then, his chances had been measurably improved when he took a job at Plant X.

It seemed to us that light might be thrown on this question if we knew what kind of jobs men aspired to and the motives behind their aspirations. For example, was a worker concerned with getting more money, acquiring higher status, finding more interesting work, or all three? Two types of questions were asked:

1. (a) What is the next job in your department you would like to go on?

(b) Why do you want this job?

2. (a) What kind of job do you hope to get on some day in your own department or in any other department?

(b) Why do you want this job?

On the first set of questions, approximately one-fifth said they were satisfied with their present jobs, and another one-sixth did not like their present jobs and wanted no other jobs in their departments. Two-thirds of the group said that they wanted some other job in the department and stated what jobs they were. Of these, fifty-six out of 114 wanted repair or utility jobs. Sixteen wished to be inspectors, fifteen wanted to become foremen, and

---

* In discussing their present jobs, workers linked transfer and promotion together, since both meant moving to a more desirable job. This linkage was natural on the assembly line, as is shown presently in this chapter.

the remaining twenty-eight wanted another production job. Almost all of the latter group wanted jobs *not* on the main line.

Significantly, less than 10 per cent volunteered increased pay as the primary reason for choosing these jobs. Most of the responses showed a clear tendency for workers to want to change the immediate content of their jobs. Many described their aspirations in this way: "On the job I want, I could do a lot of different things," or "it would give me a chance to learn more," or "it's easier, not so much work." One man put it, "I don't care — just anything except what I'm doing."

TABLE **10**

Type of Work Involved in Job Aspirations [a]

	Number of Men	Percentage
Repair-utility	51	28.3
Foreman or supervisory	38	21.1
Inspector	19	10.6
Production job other than utility or repair	15	8.3
Maintenance and tool room	14	7.8
Clerical (or other "office" work)	12	6.7
Stock, salvage, or materials handling	7	3.9
No other job (satisfied)	15	8.3
No other job (dissatisfied)	3	1.7
Does not know	6	3.3
Total	180	100.0

[a] Sample of 180 production workers.

Those persons satisfied with their present jobs seemed aware of the fact that they had positions which were "different" from most of the others. Either they were not strictly mechanically paced, or they provided variety and responsibility; or negatively, the jobs were not so physically tiring, or not so monotonous.

As to the second set of questions, concerned with future aspirations for *any jobs in the plant*, Table 10 summarizes the answers. Notice in Table 10 that more than fifty of the 180 men wanted to become repair or utility men. Interestingly enough, one-fifth of the group aspired to some kind of supervisory work, principally to the job of foreman. Except for a very small number (approximately 8 per cent), almost all of the remaining workers wanted to move away from production jobs and into maintenance, clerical or tool room jobs, scheduling, stock or salvage, and so forth.

The motivations for these choices are expressed in the typical comments below:

It's different — not doing the same thing all the time.

Can't learn anything new on the job I have now.

It's a little easier and more varied.

On the job I'd like you can see how the whole plant works.

I like to fool around with new ideas.

A foreman's job gives you different problems.

You're more like your own boss.

It's a good trade to know.

I've invested my education on skilled work like that.

In these comments and throughout the interviews, few men mentioned pay or other economic motives as reasons for wanting different jobs.* This was as true for the men who had foreman aspirations as it was for the others.

Only a few answers indicated such a factor as prestige or the desire to improve social status as a compelling motivation. On the whole, reasons fell into the following categories: (a) more variety, (b) pace not determined by a moving belt, (c) more initiative and skill demanded, (d) not as physically tiring, and (e) getting ahead — in this order. Again, most of the respondents who indicated they were satisfied with their present jobs had jobs with at least one of these characteristics.

From the above it would appear that the jobs men wanted either in their own departments or throughout Plant X as a whole were limited to certain types. The evidence suggests that the workers' chances of one day obtaining these jobs, either by

---

* Only 6.6 per cent of those aspiring to other jobs mentioned pay as a reason.

promotion or transfer, were slight. Eighty-seven per cent of the men interviewed expressed the desire and hope of one day moving to another job, but all but fifteen of these men wanted jobs which were normally held by a very small number of persons.

Eight months after the present study was completed, it was found that among 163 men of the sample still employed, ten had actually been promoted or transferred to another job classification.* According to local management, this rate of transfer or promotion was probably slightly higher than that for comparable assembly plants. Although the evidence is fragmentary, there is reason to believe that the desire for promotion or transfer was greater here than in many other occupational groups with which the authors are acquainted.

As in previous sections of this report, one of our interests is to evaluate the importance of any given job element in relation to the total job picture. So we considered two questions:

(1) How important is the question of advancement on the present job as compared with the previous one?

(2) How important is the question of advancement in comparison with other major factors such as general working conditions, economic factors, and other aspects connected with the total job?

It was found that on the previous jobs only seven men in the sample put advancement possibilities first, second, or third in importance among twenty-six favorable job factors. On the other hand, sixty-four men listed "no chance for advancement" as a first, second, or third reason for disliking their old jobs. On Plant X jobs seventeen men gave "good advancement chances" as

---

* These may be summarized as follows:
(1) Two had been promoted to salaried jobs. One had become a production foreman, and the other a nonsupervisory staff employee.
(2) Seven had been moved to production jobs in a higher job classification. Five of these became utility men.
(3) One stayed in the same pay bracket but had been transferred to another job classification.
(4) Two were moved to lesser paying jobs in production work.

either a first, second, or third reason for liking their assembly plant jobs.

These figures reinforce the evidence presented earlier and show that "no chance for advancement" was somewhat more important as a dislike factor on the previous than on the present job. How did it rate in relation to other job elements? As a "like" factor, "good chance for advancement" stood only thirteenth on previous jobs and eighth on present jobs among the twenty-seven factors. However, in the dislike columns of the check list, the negative factor, "no chance for advancement" stood third in importance on the previous job, following the two strong factors of "poor pay" and "work not steady." On the present job, this same dislike factor was tied for third place (along with uninteresting work) and followed the items, "could not set my own pace" and "job physically tiring."

Thus, the factor of advancement, or lack of it, appears of considerable importance to the men. But, as we have pointed out, the workers' motivations were not what might normally be expected. It was not promotion or transfer in order to improve one's economic or social status. Rather it was primarily a desire "to get away from the line."

SUMMARY

(1) Certain factors characteristic of the industry and mass production in general tended to limit job mobility at Plant X. These were (a) company policy, which for production reasons discouraged transfers within and among departments; (b) structure of job classifications, which was such that the pay range between lowest and highest production jobs was narrow, eliminating clear-cut and substantial promotional steps; (c) seniority system, which tended to hold men within a department or occupational group.

(2) The large majority of men expressed the desire to be promoted or transferred to other jobs. Compared with possibilities

on previous jobs, most of them considered their chances reasonably favorable.

(3) The jobs aspired to were not usually other straight production jobs. Rather they were the jobs of foreman, utilityman, repairman, maintenance, inspection or clerical worker, and others.

(4) The principal reason for wanting transfer or promotion was not as a rule the desire to improve wages or social status, but the desire to get away from present production jobs. This was especially true among those who worked on the line. Pacing, repetition, and physical fatigue — in other words, those features of the job which have already been described as undesirable — were primary reasons for wanting to change jobs.

(5) An analysis of the jobs men wanted showed these jobs to be held by relatively few persons. Turnover on such jobs was lower than on most production jobs.

(6) In the total present job picture, as revealed in the check lists, it was found that lack of advancement opportunities was of real importance to one out of every five men.

10 MASS PRODUCTION CHARACTER-ISTICS AND HUMAN BEHAVIOR

We began this study with a breakdown of the mass production characteristics of the assembly man's job — machine pacing, repetitiveness, and four others. In most of the following chapters have been recorded qualitative comments which sharply reflect a dislike of these characteristics, especially if they found expression in the "immediate job" or imposed restrictions on social interaction. Mass production characteristics, in short, appear to have strongly influenced the worker's *attitude* toward his job, and in a majority of instances influenced his attitude unfavorably.

But did these characteristics influence or determine actual *behavior?* Is there valid evidence that a worker on a job which has extreme mass production characteristics acts any differently (whatever he may *say*) from a worker on a job without them? Every investigator of human behavior knows the importance of the distinction made, a distinction between verbalizations of emotion and the same emotion resulting in action. Similarly, every factory manager knows the crucial difference between a "gripe" and the overt act of walking off the job. Griping is often referred to by military men as an "inalienable right of the American soldier." Experience shows that the heavy griper is not necessarily a bad soldier — or an inefficient worker. For these and other reasons, we have sought evidence of behavioral correlations with mass production characteristics.

Indirect evidence may be found in the grievance record at Plant X (cf. Chapter XI, "The Worker and the Union"). A substantial number of workers filed grievances centering on "job standards," that is, on questions relating directly to number of operations, mechanical pacing, and other mass production characteristics. There were many more such grievances than there were in the commoner complaint areas of wages or seniority. Thus workers *acted* through the grievance machinery in response to certain characteristics of their jobs which they said they disliked.

Certain studies in English factories * have shown that extreme repetitiveness reduces the productivity of the individual worker. He produces more when there is some measure of variety in his job. Is it possible, then, to relate the productivity of workers in Plant X to repetitiveness, mechanical pacing, and so forth? In our opinion, no. Individual productivity in American automobile assembly operations, under present conditions, is not measured with any degree of accuracy. Rather, it is common practice to set merely a minimum standard, after which the conveyor wholly determines the pace, and hence the productivity, of the worker. Accordingly, we have rejected variations in productivity as a measure of overt behavior.

There remain, however, two important ways of "behaving" which commonly indicate how a worker feels about his job. He can stay away periodically, or he can quit the job altogether. In figures collected by the Bureau of Labor Statistics for automobile assembly plants, there is sufficient data, in our opinion, for the general hypothesis of a connection between mass production jobs and a high quit rate. For such plants,** the number of

---

* S. Wyatt and J. A. Fraser, *The Effects of Monotony in Work, A Preliminary Inquiry*, Industrial Fatigue Research Board, Report no. 56 (London: His Majesty's Stationery Office, 1929). Other relevant British reports issued by the board are Vernon and Wyatt, *The Extent and Effects of Variety in Repetitive Work*, Report no. 26 (1929), and Wyatt and Fraser, *The Comparative Effects of Variety and Uniformity in Work*, Report no. 52 (1928). These studies had been preceded by a large number of industrial reports upon physiological fatigue as related to productivity conducted by the British Government during the First World War.

** Recorded in the Bureau of Labor Statistics as the "motor vehicles, bodies and trailer industry," as distinguished from the "motor vehicle parts and accessories industry."

employees (per 100) who quit in 1949 was higher than for any of the other forty-one durable goods manufacturing industries listed.* The rate was 2.7 as compared with an average of 1.5 for the other durable goods manufacturing industries.**

With these facts in mind, we sought in the present study to analyze the record of quits for Plant X. A breakdown of the quit records for production and non-production workers revealed a significant relationship between the kinds of work men performed and their overt behavior. In the January-June 1949 period, the number of employees (per 100) who quit was almost twice as high (3.0) among *production* workers (that is, men on the assembly line) as among *non-production* workers (1.6), those performing maintenance, stock, salvage, and other *non-*mass production jobs.

We then focused on our immediate sample of production workers. Two types of rating scales were clearly called for if possible correlations were to be sought: one for absenteeism, and one for job characteristics suitable for application to all workers in our sample. Did we have sufficient data to construct such scales? After a thorough study of the company's absentee records and of all job characteristics as reflected in our interviews, we concluded that we did. Scales were then constructed as follows.

Each worker's record was studied for the year 1949. Notations were made as to the number of times a worker was late, the number of days absent, and the reasons given. Then a simple rating scale was developed wherein one point was given for a single lateness, two points for being absent one or two days because of "illness," and three points for absences for which "no reason" was given.† Then each worker was scored. The results

---

* "Monthly Labor Turn-Over Rates (Per 100 Employees) in Selected Groups and Industries," Table B-2, *Monthly Labor Review*, vols. 68–70.
** The rate was also higher than for any one of the non-durable goods industries and for any one of the nonmanufacturing industries (except copper mining) in the country during this period.
† A single and a two-day absence due to sickness were given the same scoring, two points. Consecutive sickness absences beyond two days were not counted. The employment and medical departments maintained a

for our sample of 180 showed a range from zero, those with a perfect record for the year, to thirty-six, an extremely poor record. Median scores fell between six and seven points.

The rating scale for job characteristics was somewhat more complex, but not difficult to construct. Consider the typical characteristic, repetitiveness. It was obvious that a range in the degree of repetitiveness obtained for any given job. A single-operation job is highly repetitive; a ten-operation job is considerably less repetitive. Similarly, a range between extremes is discernible in other mass production job characteristics. In the characteristic, mechanical pacing, for example, a job on the main line is generally more strictly paced than a job on a sub-assembly line, and a job on a sub-assembly line more than a "bank building" job. It was found possible to work out a three-point range for six typical mass production job factors, with 0 representing the greatest embodiment of the mass production characteristic, 2 representing the least embodiment, and 1 representing a mean point between the two.

The following factors were chosen and scaled: (1) degree of repetitiveness; (2) degree of mechanical pacing; (3) skill as measured by length of learning time; (4) frequency of break in job routine; (5) frequency of social interaction; and (6) size of interacting group.

A word of explanation on the choice of the six factors: They were chosen as being those most susceptible to a quantitative expression of range. Notice that the first three, repetitiveness, mechanical pacing, and minimum skill (as measured by learning time), are the first three of the familiar six characteristics which

---

thorough system of checking on extended illnesses. Since our interest was in willful absence not accounted for by sickness, the above point system was adopted to minimize absenteeism due to sickness. Also not scored were leaves of absence for illness or for other excused reasons and absences of union officers when on official business. A somewhat similar weighting system was used by John B. Fox and Jerome F. Scott in their study of East Coast metal-working shops (*Absenteeism: Management's Problem*, Harvard Research Studies No. 29, Cambridge, Harvard University Bureau of Business Research, 1943).

have been employed throughout this book. The fourth, frequency of break in job routine, was found as our study progressed to be generally mentioned by our sample as one gauge of the desirability or undesirability of a job at Plant X. No man, of course, can leave a strictly paced conveyor job for any purpose — to go to the toilet, get a drink of water, or take a "breather" — without signaling for and obtaining a relief man. As a consequence, on strictly paced jobs there was often a low frequency in "breaks." The fifth and sixth factors, frequency of interaction and size of interacting group, are included as measures of the amount permitted or the restriction imposed upon social interaction by mass production techniques.*

Using the above factors, for any one worker a score of zero to twelve was possible. Take, for example, a man's job where every one of the six factors appeared in its most extreme form. Thus, if a man's work pace was determined solely by the moving conveyor, if he performed only one operation, if his learning time was less than one week, if he could rarely "take a break," if he had little actual and little potential interaction with other workers, his total score was the sum of all the zeros, or zero. If, on the other hand, the job factors were the least extreme, several operations not on a moving conveyor, a considerable learning time period, frequent break in routine, frequent interaction, a larger work group, a score of twelve was possible. The median score for all workers fell between five and six points.

Having constructed these two scales for 175 workers,** we studied the relationship of one to the other. The result is shown in Table 11. The first vertical column (Below Median Job Factor Score) represents those workers who had jobs with the more

* There were, the reader may remember, three other characteristics included in our original six — predetermination of tools and techniques, minute subdivision of the product worked on, and surface attention. As to predetermination, this characteristic applies with little variation to all jobs on a final assembly line, and for that reason it is not included as a range factor in our rating scale. As to subdivision of product worked on and surface mental attention, our data were insufficient to establish a range for these factors.

** Records on full sample of 180 were incomplete.

extreme mass production characteristics. Notice that the great majority of this group of eighty-nine had the poorer absentee record. The second column represents those workers who had jobs with less extreme mass production characteristics. Here a reverse tendency is shown. Of the eighty-six in the total, only thirty-two were absent more than average, while fifty-four had a good absentee record.

TABLE 11

Absenteeism Related to Job Factors
(175 Workers) [a]

	Below Median Job Factor Score (0–5 points)	Above Median Job Factor Score (6–12 points)	Total [b]
Lower than Median Absentee Record (0–6 points)	35	54	89
Higher than Median Absentee Record (7 or more points)	54	32	86
Total [b]	89	86	175

[a] Records on full sample of 180 were not available.
[b] Line and column totals do not divide exactly at the median of 175. In each case the nearest point score figure to the median was used.

Using the standard chi square test of association, it was found that $x^2 = 9.71$ at the one degree of freedom level. The probability (P) of the figures given in this table occurring by chance is less than one in 100. Thus a clear association between absenteeism and mass production characteristics was found. Men with highly repetitive jobs, conveyor paced, and so forth, were far more likely to take time off from work than those whose jobs did not contain such job characteristics.

Further reinforcement of the tie beween behavior and mass production characteristics was found when turnover records were examined. Among our sample of 175 workers, twenty-two men had voluntarily quit work at Plant X between 1949 and 1951. These do not include men who had left for medical reasons, military or medical leaves of absences, those who had died, or those who had been laid off because of reduction in operations. An additional four had been discharged for disciplinary reasons.

Of the twenty-two men, fourteen had lower than median scores on the job factors described above. Eight with above median job factor scores had left Plant X. Of the four who had been discharged, three had below and one had above median scores. The average for the sample in job factor points was 5.80. The average score for those who had left was 4.53.

These are small figures on which to base an assumption about the relationship between the nature of a worker's immediate job and his chances of ending his employment. Yet a tendency is suggested. It is to be noted that almost twice the number of workers who had less desirable job factors left work as compared with workers whose job factors were favorable.

SUMMARY

(1) This chapter seeks to answer the question: Is there any correlation between mass production characteristics and overt human behavior?

(2) The hypothesis that such a correlation exists is suggested by the fact that the quit rate for assembly plants in the automobile industry is higher than for all manufacturing industries and for all but one nonmanufacturing industry.

(3) It was found possible to score production jobs at Plant X in terms of job factors indicating which jobs had mass production characteristics in their most extreme form, which in their least extreme form, and which occupied a middle range. It was also possible out of Plant X records to construct an absenteeism score for each worker.

(4) By comparing scores, a correlation was found to exist between absenteeism and mass production characteristics. Workers whose jobs showed "a high mass production score" were absent more often than workers whose jobs had a low mass production score.

(5) Quit records for our sample showed that nearly twice as many workers left the jobs with extreme mass production characteristics as left jobs with moderate mass production characteristics.

Thus there were strong indications that mass production characteristics at Plant X had been reflected, not simply in attitude and opinion, but in overt behavior.

11 THE WORKERS AND THE UNION

Although our focus of interest in this study is not on union-management relations, the union is clearly relevant to a discussion of job elements at many points. Wages and the wage structure in Company X were molded in part by the union's activities; seniority was a factor in promotion and transfer, and questions of individual work load and job duties were at times subjects of disagreement between union and management. In short, the union was an important conditioning factor in the total job picture at Plant X.

In this chapter we will look first at the over-all status of union-management relations at Plant X, including an analysis of the grievance record. Then, we will turn to interview material for the actual attitudes of workers toward their union, quantitatively and qualitatively expressed. Finally, we shall look at the rating scale for an answer to the question: How important did the union seem to the workers as a reason for liking their jobs in comparison with other job elements? Throughout the chapter we shall be trying to throw light on a question which has been asked before but never satisfactorily answered: What effect or influence have the mass production methods of the assembly line had on the role and activities of the union?

We turn first to a brief review of the facts and to an appraisal of the status of industrial relations at Plant X. The union was organized without hostile incident, and a relatively friendly atmosphere has prevailed since the beginning. A United Automobile Workers local of the CIO was formed shortly after plant operations began, with the active backing of representatives from the international union. Following an NLRB representation election,[*] the national contract was put into effect and agreements negotiated locally on wages and seniority.

For the corporation of which Plant X is a part, bargaining relations began for this whole industrial area with this particular plant. For many of the men unionism was a brand-new experience. Less than 2 per cent had been either members of the UAW or employees of the corporation prior to taking a job in this plant. Half of the workers had never been members of any union.

The job of organizing the plant was carried out in an orderly and businesslike fashion, and there was no strike for recognition. At the time of this study, the summer of 1949, 80 per cent of the workers in our sample were found to be union members, and in March, 1950, an even larger percentage of the local voted in favor of a union shop. Attendance at union meetings, while not unusually high, was at least as great as that for most other locals in the industry.

A brief walkout occurred at Plant X during the period of our study, but it hardly interrupted what seemed to the investigators a stable and workable union-management relationship. During an unusually hot spell in the summer of 1949, a group of 110 men left their jobs, walked out of the plant during the lunch period, and failed to return for the duration of the shift. The walkout, which had not been authorized by the union, necessitated closing the entire plant for the balance of the shift and sending all employees home. Shortly after, eleven of these men were discharged. These eleven were new employees and had not completed their ninety-day trial period. The employees with seniority, most of whom were union members, were later given written reprimands.

Whatever the merits of the case from a contractual point of view, most of the workers in the plant disagreed with this action by plant management, and during the period of discussion over the issue, over three hundred men who had not yet joined the union went to the union office and signed up. A strike vote was

[*] The vote was 980 for the union and ninety-eight against it.

taken in which nine out of ten voted to authorize a protest strike.

After a series of meetings between representatives of the local and national union organizations and representatives of the company's local and central offices, the matter was peaceably settled. The men who had been discharged were reinstated, but warned that such a walkout was directly contrary to procedures established by the union contract.

From the union's point of view, the strike's net effect, as one officer described it, was a "shot in the arm" for the union. On the other hand, the company expressed the belief that the incident had made it clear that any similar illegal action would not be condoned, and that if one should occur, the men could expect stronger disciplinary action.

We have given a brief account of this work stoppage because it marked the first and only critical episode in local union-management relations. In order to gauge whether it had influenced the character of our interview material, we compared answers to questions before the strike with answers afterward. More workers favored the union after the strike than had before, but otherwise there was no discernible pattern of difference.

We turn now to the grievance record for Plant X during the six-months period preceding our study. It was on the whole a good record, comparing favorably with other plants of a similar character within Corporation X.

During these months eighty-four formal grievances were settled.* In the first step, eight were settled between the worker (or committeeman) and the foreman, forty between the committeeman and the department sunperintendent. In the second step, eighteen grievances were settled between top local management and the local union. In the third step, seventeen went to the appeal board. In the fourth step, only one case came up for settlement by the umpire.

For this study of the particular work environment of an

* These, of course, do not include the larger number of complaints which were resolved before going into formal grievance procedures.

assembly line, the *kind* of grievances recorded is of special interest. Table 12 lists the general subject matter of all cases settled during the six months prior to this study. We believe Table 12 adds some supporting evidence to what has been suggested in previous chapters regarding sources of job satisfaction or dissatisfaction. For example, we had found relatively

TABLE **12**

Grievances Settled During Period of January–June, 1949, by Subject

Type of Grievance	Number of Cases
Discipline [a]	23
Production standards	14
Foremen working	10
Promotions	9
Wages [b]	7
Transfers	5
Working conditions	4
Overtime equalization	3
Seniority	3
Criticism of supervision	2
Grievance procedure	2
Shift hours	1
Representation	1
Total	84

[a] "Discipline," as pointed out below, refers to grievances arising from infringements of rules.

[b] The category of "Wages," fifth in number of grievances, comprises disputes over individual job rates, not general wage levels.

little dissatisfaction over hours, general working conditions, wages, and supervision. These same items are low on the list of grievances. Grievances concerning promotions and transfers were more frequent than those just mentioned. Since a majority of workers strongly desired promotion or transfer from their present jobs, this is not surprising.

Grievances over production standards were second in the list of thirteen grievance categories. Here is the area of the "immediate job." These grievances involved individual or group standards of expected production within a given time period.

The disputes were between the individual's opinion of his work capacity, in relation to the speed of the line, and the work expected of him by management. We have stressed that a principal source of dissatisfaction among workers at Plant X stemmed from the immediate job itself — the machine pace and the lack of individual control over this pace. The high number of formal grievances on production standards, by reflecting resistance to standards as related to the machine-paced conveyor, appears to support this finding.

The largest number of grievances concerned discipline. The significance of this fact is hard to appraise in the light of previous findings, since most of the persons actually involved were not in our sample. A large number of the discipline cases arose from excessive absenteeism. Concerning the causes of absenteeism at Plant X, management representatives offered two explanations: (1) that many of the men were getting much higher wages than formerly and felt "they could afford to loaf a day now and again"; (2) that many men were used to more perfunctory attendance on their former jobs. Local union officers offered another explanation: that absenteeism was traceable to dissatisfactions with factors in the immediate job. The workers themselves were not asked to discuss specifically the question of unauthorized absenteeism. Nevertheless, they occasionally remarked that men stayed out sometimes in order to "take a break from the grind." In the last chapter we gave our evidence for a marked correlation between mass production characteristics and . absenteeism.

Looking at the grievance record as a whole, it may be said that:

(1) The total number of grievances for the six-months period was not high considering the newness of the local bargaining relationship.

(2) Few cases went beyond local management and the local union. Since the opening the plant, only one case was referred to the umpire.

(3) Few grievances concerned working conditions, hours, wages, or supervision, the subjects which tend to predominate in many collective bargaining relationships.

(4) On the other hand, disliked elements in the immediate job appeared reflected in the proportionately larger number of cases concerned with production standards.

We turn now to the attitudes of Plant X workers toward their union and to the relationship between these attitudes and workers' job satisfaction or dissatisfaction. In our interviews the men were asked to tell what they thought about the union and why. Responses were then rated as (1) generally favorable toward the union, (2) neutral or mixed, and (3) generally unfavorable.

Of the workers in our sample 119 (66.1 per cent) expressed themselves as being generally favorable. Another forty-five (25 per cent) were either neutral or mixed in attitude. Sixteen (just under 9 per cent) said they were not in favor of the union.

(1) FAVORABLE ATTITUDE TOWARD UNION

The favorable responses may be grouped into three categories. To a number of men the union was an instrument of protection. Another type of response centered on the youth of the organization and pointed out that although "weak" the union was growing stronger. Still another group discussed in favorable terms the walkout of July, 1949 (described above), and the strike vote. Many of these men appeared more inclined to favor the union as a result of this incident. Following is a series of quotations representing the differing attitudes which cover a wide variety of subjects:

GENERALLY FAVORABLE ATTITUDE TOWARD THE UNION

Yes, it's a pretty good union. It tries to back the men; it's with them.

The union's a good thing. Without it you haven't got a chance.

I'm going in. I've seen what the union can do. It saves a lot of men from being fired and from working their hearts out.

The union is a wonderful thing. The small men can't talk in a big company and can't go to the top man.

The union is very good. At first we were making only twenty-five cars an hour, which of course is low and what you might expect with a new plant. But now we're making forty-five, and we don't know where they'll stop. We need protection and the union gives it.

It's necessary to have representation. Everybody can't go to see the supervisor at once.

I'm not a union man as a rule, but when you work for an outfit this big, you couldn't do without one.

The union is necessary with a big concern. It's the only way a working man can get anything. The union here is not as strong as it could be. The men don't realize that they need a union. The union's not bad. It's the men; they don't care.

I never filed a grievance or made a complaint, but you always like to know you have somebody to speak for you.

The union is a good "racket." It kind of holds the boys together. If we have trouble, the committeeman will iron it out.

The union is the only thing a man has to defend himself. Without it a man wouldn't be worth a nickel.

The union is a wonderful thing. Without it, if you get into any difficulty, you're licked. In the union there's strength.

COMMENTS ON THE NEWNESS OF THE UNION

Yes, I'm in the union, although it is too young to really get organized right. But I'm in favor of unions.

The union saved my job. It's getting more powerful every day.

It's a green union, but it will be good in time. It just needs more experience.

So far the fellows are not behind the union. We have to have a strong union to get anywhere down there.

The union is starting to do something now. The trouble is with the men; they don't bother. The union should be the men and not a few officials.

The union has accomplished some things. They're still weak, but getting stronger.

The union will be all right after it gets experience. It's new, like the plant. It's making mistakes, but learning.

I think the union is O.K., but it could be improved a lot. The union was new and had no following; that was the trouble.

It's like every other union. It's nice to have. Even a poor union is better than none at all. This one is young, but it's trying to help the men.

THE UNION AND THE STRIKE VOTE

I didn't think much of the union until last summer. Now I think more of it.

Up until recently the union had no backing. Since the strike vote we've had the backing and we showed the company.

MISCELLANEOUS AND GENERAL COMMENTS

Yes, the union's good, although it's the first union I've been in.

Although I belong to the union, I don't get too close to it, or I'd spend too much time in it.

It should be a closed shop. The union's a good thing.

(2) NEUTRAL OR MIXED ATTITUDES TOWARD THE UNION

The following group of quotations are taken from those interviews in which men expressed mixed or neutral opinions. These comments do not fall into set patterns as do the generally favorable comments above, but they do contain elements found in both the generally favorable groups and the generally unfavorable groups to be recorded later.

We didn't have much of a union last year. It came in September. It's strong enough, but the majority of the men can't seem to find their gripes (express themselves or claim grievances). They are afraid of making fools of themselves.

The union is O.K., except that it hasn't done anything about the speed yet. The one thing I fear is a walkout. I was in one once, and I'm not eager for another. I have a family.

The union is all right. I think it could be better, bucking for vacations and things like that.

The union protects the men, but it also protects the shirker as well as the earnest worker.

I've never been fond of unions, but if it really helps the working man, I'm for it. It has its good points.

The union is all right, but it should do something to prove to the guys that it has more power. If it did, more of them would join up. [Interview was before the walkout incident.]

I'm not too interested in the union, but I think it's needed.

I never thought much about a union, but you have to have somebody represent you or you won't get anywhere.

The union is new. Being new, the men at the head of it are kind of lost. The company knows where it is going. The local union doesn't, but in time they will straighten it out.

The union is all right. There are a few agitators in there. They don't think before they shout.

In appraising the significance of some of these comments, it should be remembered that a good critic is often a good friend. For that reason, as many pro-union men may perhaps be counted among those making mixed comments as among the workers registering a blanket approval.

(3) GENERALLY UNFAVORABLE ATTITUDES TOWARD THE UNION

The remaining men showed strong dislike of the union because it was not functioning as they thought a union should.

The union hasn't done anything for the men. It said it would improve working conditions. So far they haven't. If I were for it, I'd be a strong union man. If it were good, I'd just as soon join. A lot of odd guys join it and run it down. They find everything wrong with it. Unless it's better, why join?

I have the very lowest thoughts possible about the union. It is useless — the union hardly ever wins — only when the company lets them win. I think the company is more or less fair in its judgments.

The union is no damned good. Look at the ignorance of the officers. It's a racket. The international representative is a sorry character.

I dropped out of the union. The committeemen are green and don't know anything. They've got a "rocket."

It would appear from these qualitative remarks that, except for a vociferous minority, a majority of the men favored the union and that its role at Plant X was an important one.

As with other job elements, we turn for a comparative evaluation to our rating scale. What was the relative importance of the union, as the workers themselves saw it, compared with other elements such as pace, working conditions, and so forth, in the total job?

Only two men in the sample of 180 workers interviewed gave the union as their first reason for liking their jobs at Plant X. The great majority checked as their first reasons either good pay, steady work, or good working hours. The union was checked by thirty workers as the second or third "most important reason for liking the job." In the dislike column three workers gave "union in the plant" as a reason for disliking their present jobs.

What was the principal service or function performed by the union at Plant X which had won the support and favorable comment of a majority of the workers? The backing accorded the union was the more striking to the authors in view of the previous experience of the men. Less than half, as we noted earlier, had been members of any union before coming to Plant X. Only two had been members of the United Automobile Workers. None had been officers of any union. What, then, explained the fact that a majority of the work force had shifted rapidly from a neutral or non-union to a fairly active pro-union position?

In seeking an answer, the authors examined the usual reasons why workers join unions, or why after joining they continue to give a union their support. Was it any one of the following? (1) wages; (2) job security; (3) hours; (4) working conditions; (5) abuse of authority by foremen or by other supervisors; or

(6) acts of discrimination by management against workers because of color, nationality, or political or union affiliation.

None of these reasons appeared to be applicable as explanations of why workers supported the union at Plant X. Our examination of the several elements of their jobs showed that in fact a large majority of workers were well satisfied with wages, job security, hours, and the other items mentioned. As to Point 6, during the period of our study no case of discrimination by management was reported.

Is there any other explanation? We have noted from time to time throughout this inquiry evidences of on-the-job "frustration." Some workers were able to counterbalance a lack of personal satisfaction in their immediate work experience with other factors, social interaction, for example, or the high wages they were making, but others were less able to do so. In our discussion of relations with supervision, social or functional contacts by workers with any one above the rank of foreman were tenuous. Thus the average worker was unable to identify himself either with the work he did with his hands or with those responsible for managing it. As a hypothesis, therefore, we suggest that the union met in part the psychological and social needs which work in the plant had created. That unions often do play such a role for their members has now been accepted as a commonplace, but here the point of interest is that these needs sprang directly from the particular characteristics of a mass production work environment. As might be expected, the interviews show that most workers counted on their union for its regular services as their bargaining agent. But they also suggest an emotional as well as an economic dimension in the workers' attitudes. In other words, for a considerable number of Plant X workers the union appeared as a kind of psychological bulwark against pace and boredom and against the bigness and impersonality of management.

SUMMARY

(1) Soon after its opening, Plant X was organized without incident by the United Automobile Workers of America — CIO. Union-management relations from the beginning were stable with one minor interruption in the summer of 1949.

(2) The grievance record, especially for a newly organized plant, was a good one, with few cases going beyond the local grievance machinery for settlement.

(3) An analysis of the type of grievance processed confirms earlier findings as to what caused job satisfaction and what caused job dissatisfaction in Plant X. The record reflects the disliked elements of the immediate job, especially in cases dealing with production standards.

(4) Although on the rating scale the workers did not give the union prominence as a specific reason either for liking or for disliking their Plant X jobs, their qualitative remarks showed two-thirds of the sample to be favorable to the union.

(5) The nature of workers' comments together with other evidence suggests that, in addition to its usual bargaining functions, the union met a psychological need by counterbalancing in part the sense of impersonality and anonymity men felt in their work.

12 THE WORKER LOOKS AT COMPANY X

In addition to questions that dealt with specific elements of the worker's job situation at Plant X, we asked one question designed to throw light on what he thought of the company or corporation as a whole. In the undirected part of our preliminary interviews it was found that nearly every worker expressed an opinion about the company and almost always in terms of what Plant X or Company X was doing for him or for some other employee, whether much or little. Accordingly, we framed a question as follows: "Do you think the company (1) does all it can for the men? (2) does something, but not all it could do? (3) doesn't do much of anything?"

(1) Twenty (11.1 per cent) of the 180 men who were interviewed said that the company did all it could for the men.

(2) Sixty-five (36.1 per cent) said that the company did something for the men but not all it could.

(3) Ninety-four (52.2 per cent) said that the company did not do much of anything for the men.*

The age and education of the workers interviewed appear to have had some bearing on these attitudes toward the company. For example, looking at the two groups who expressed completely favorable and completely unfavorable attitudes toward the company, it was found that older workers more frequently, younger workers less frequently, expressed favorable attitudes toward the company.

As to educational level and the two extremes of company attitude, there appeared to be some tendency for workers with more

---

* One respondent gave an indeterminate answer.

education to have less favorable opinions about the company.

These very general summaries of attitudes become more meaningful when we turn to the qualitative comments which workers gave in explanation of them.

Typical of those who thought "the company does all it can for the men" were such comments as:

The company has really helped a lot. They have brought security to a great many men who never had it before.

They're pretty good with the men — lavatories, bathrooms, showers, and a good hospital.

The company looked out for me first rate. I cut my hand. They took care of me and gave me a light job. They used me very well.

Under the existing conditions I would say the company was doing everything possible for the men. After all, they are running a business. It's the work that's rough, but it's a good outfit.

Turn now to the second group, those who said the company "does something, but not all it could do." This group might be called the mixed favorable and unfavorable grounp. The positive side of their comments covered a variety of factors such as high pay, job security, good working conditions, and so forth. On the negative side, a majority of comments were tied to two themes: (1) disliked characteristics of the assembly line, for which the company as a rule was blamed; (2) alleged company disregard of the individual. Some combined a favorable attitude to the company with an unfavorable one toward the assembly line:

Sometimes the company does what it can, sometimes not. Departments are different. Some departments realize the men are human and that the line is no fun.

The company has done a lot for me. They asked for blood donors on the bulletin board and they saved my daughter's life — and saved me paying for the blood. But the work itself is a steady grind.

The only thing bothering everybody is the speed. They ought to slow down or hire more men.

They could do more to improve conditions, and it would pay them. For instance, they could give scheduled breaks during the day.

I like the medical service they give. Also, the job gives me better living conditions; that's the main thing. But the monotony of the job and the speed of the line are bad. It doesn't bother me so much now, but it will in ten years. I'd rather work for less at less speed.

Below are remarks of those whose unfavorable comments concerned the company's disregard of the individual:

It's a big outfit; they're strict. They can't deal with an individual. They can only consider groups.

The company tries to do some things, but it wants to get the cars out. They are first, and the men are second.

As far as hospital treatment goes, the company goes all the way. But they treat the men like one of the machines.

The company tries to please everybody, but is is impossible to please a huge group.

The company gives the men a good break often. It doesn't do everything, but it does more than many large companies.

We turn now to the comments of the third group, those who said the company "doesn't do much of anything" for the men. A similar pattern of criticism emerges here, but in phrases carrying more emotional impact. As before, the majority of unfavorable comments were concerned either with the workers' dislike for assembly line work or with the company's alleged disregard of the individual. Typical comments of those who disliked the line were the following:

The men on the line have too much work for the time allowed. The company just cares for production, not the men at all.

The company is against the worker. It changes the lunch hour or cuts it off so that a line can catch up. The line goes so fast that guys can't keep up, especially new guys. This results in inferior work, so the company gets behind. Overtime and short lunch hours result.

The worst is the pressure. It's like on a dog-sled. As soon as the whistle blows, they yell "Mush," and away you go producing cars. The company should at least give us a five-minute break. Or the pace could be slower. The **only** good thing the company has is a hospital, and that is really good.

That group of workers who were generally unfavorable to the company but who criticized it in more general terms for what appeared to them a disregard of themselves as individuals commented as follows:

I'm left with the impression that the company doesn't think so much of the individual. If it did, they wouldn't have a production line like this one.

The place is run like the Army. They should think more about the men than the product they put out. They could do a lot more.

You're just a number to them. They number the stock, and they number you.

There is a different feeling in this plant. It's much bigger than people around here have ever seen. It's just like the kid who goes up to a grownup man and starts talking to him. There doesn't seem to be a friendly feeling. At the plant I used to work in there was a different attitude. Everyone spoke to everyone else. Different feeling. Nobody goes to other departments in this plant. The understanding could be better, happier and much easier. Here a man is just so much horsepower. If he's no good, they just kick him out. You're just a cog in the wheel.

As long as they get the cars out, they don't give a damn for the man.

It's a big concern. They are out to make money, and they don't care how they do it. They don't care how the men feel; they only care about money. If I were in their position, I'd probably be that way too, but they ignore the way the men feel.

The company just thinks of the men as robots. If they get the cars out, they don't care what happens to the men. The bigger the company, the less they do for the men. The engineers never talk to us except on business.

Here is angry criticism in words charged with emotion. The reader will remember that as we examined one by one the several

elements in the total job situation at Plant X the attitude of a
majority of our sample toward each of the elements, except immediate job content, was favorable. Even when criticisms were
made, the attitude of the critic was as a rule balanced and constructive, and the words used were not strongly emotional. Why
then this burst of hostile feeling against the company on the part
of a substantial group?

Part of the explanation might lie in the actual formulation of
the question to which we have been recording answers. It should
be noticed that the workers were *not* asked to give a balanced
judgment about their jobs as a whole. Rather they were asked
this simple question: "Do you think Company X does all it can
for the men . . . ?" Thus it may be argued that had they been
asked to weigh and evaluate their total job situation the answer
would have been more "reasonable." However that may be, we
believe it is significant that this or any other question released
such emotional comments touching the two themes, assembly
line work and the alleged failure of the company to treat the
workers as individuals. These sentiments were clearly in the
workers' minds and ready to come to the surface at an appropriate stimulus.

Notice in particular the different feeling-tone with which
workers have discussed any *particular* element or person connected with their jobs, even the disliked aspects of the immediate
job, and the feeling-tone here exhibited in some of the unfavorable comments about Company X. On the whole, when a worker
talked about any particular job phase or element, or about any
particular member of supervision or management, he was favorable in comment, *or* controlled in criticism. Even when discussing
the pace of the line and repetitiveness, many workers made practical and very specific suggestions. Often in the same sentence
they balanced what they liked and disliked about their jobs. When
workers turned to discuss the company or the corporation, however, day to day irritations and frustrations appeared to coalesce
into hostile criticism. It would appear that here was the psycho-

logical process of frustration passing into aggression, in this case, "verbal aggression," and focusing not upon any known individual but upon the company as the agent responsible for what they did not like. Individuals appear to have been exonerated because they were thought of as "not responsible."

The fact that the assembly line was in sharp contrast with previous work experience for many, and perhaps stirred a sense of cultural values at variance with its principles, may account for some of the intensity of the emotions expressed. Whatever the explanation, the fact and intensity of the frustration of a considerable number of workers seems clear. In order to eliminate some of its causes, certain suggestions offered by the workers themselves will be reviewed and discussed in the next and final chapter of this inquiry.

13 CONCLUSIONS

We shall review the findings of this study under the following headings:

(1) The impact of mass production characteristics on the individual worker through his immediate job:

    (a) Summary of evidence.

    (b) Review of what the workers say should be done about it.

(2) The impact of mass production characteristics on social organization and social structure:

    (a) Summary of evidence.

    (b) Review of suggestions as implied by Plant X workers.

(3) The problem of mass production in perspective.

IMPACT OF MASS PRODUCTION CHARACTERISTICS ON THE INDIVIDUAL WORKER

Roughly 10 per cent of our sample of workers preferred or were indifferent to jobs with basic mass production characteristics such as mechanical pacing, repetitiveness, and so forth. The great majority expressed in varying degrees a dislike of these features of their job situations at Plant X.

Because of the considerable importance attached to this finding in itself, as well as to its implications, we here review in some detail the evidence upon which it is based. Direct evidence has consisted of qualitative comments, and their quantitative summary, upon that element in the total work situation we have called "the immediate job." We record also correlations between mass production characteristics and overt behavior. Indirect evidence has consisted of the comparative ratings by the workers and their indirect references to the immediate job appearing throughout the inquiry whenever any element in the total job situation was discussed.

Consider the direct testimony. We were continually struck by the acute awareness of workers of all factors of immediate job content, and how in discussion they discriminated among them. If a man was on a strictly paced, highly repetitive job, and belonged to the majority who did not like it, he said so bluntly. If he had been transferred off the line onto a less strictly paced or a less repetitive job, he reported this circumstance with satisfaction. In short, a majority specifically stated that they liked their jobs to the degree to which they lacked repetitiveness, mechanical pacing, or related characteristics. On the other hand, they *disliked them to the degree to which they embodied these mass production characteristics.*

Turning now to the indirect testimony, the reader will recall that, as each of the other job elements was examined, evidence on likes and dislikes appeared tangentially and in a great variety of forms. This may be reviewed briefly as follows:

When the worker discussed his *relations with other workers* and reported social interaction, such as joking, gossiping, or general conversation, he mentioned them chiefly as a fortunate counterbalance and compensation for the disliked features of immediate job content.

As to the economic aspects of his job, *pay and security* both were strong *like* factors. What is here significant is that the worker himself frequently juxtaposed these likes with the strongest of his dislikes, that is, unpleasant features of the immediate job.

By comparing his attitude toward these elements on both his present and his previous job, our findings become clear. As Table 13 shows, former jobs were disliked for economic reasons and generally liked because of the jobs. The reverse is true for jobs at Plant X. Only one man considered an economic factor as the principal reason for not liking his present job. Only seven among the entire sample of 180 put an immediate job factor first as a reason for liking the job.

As to *relations with supervision*, a large majority of workers rated their foremen high. No worker blamed front-line supervision, or indeed any member of local management, for the most disliked features of his job. Why? One part of the answer is certainly that management had done an unusually good job in both the selection and the training of section foremen. The other part of the answer derives, we believe, from the men's comments ex-

TABLE **13**

Number of Men Listing an Economic or Immediate Job Factor as Primary Reason for Liking or Disliking Previous and Present Jobs

Factors	Likes		Dislikes	
	Previous	Present	Previous	Present
Economic	54	147	81	1
Immediate job content	53	7	18	96

onerating front-line supervision. They said in effect that their immediate bosses were not to be held responsible for the unpleasant features of assembly line work. They merely "did what they were told." Blame for what was disliked was shifted to the company or the corporation as such.

The good *working conditions* at Plant X were appreciated and praised by a majority in our sample. But favorable comments were often qualified by statements that good working conditions did not counterbalance the drudgery of the line.

Finally, regarding *promotion and transfer*, a very large number of workers aspired to other jobs and thought their chances at Plant X good, certainly better than with their previous employers. But the basic motivation for wanting promotion or transfer was rarely more money, or prestige, or advancement, as might have been expected. Rather, as revealed by an unusually large number of qualitative comments, it was the desire to replace a paced, repetitive, or otherwise unpleasant job. The most popular jobs were those of utilitymen, foremen, and repairmen — those resembling line jobs least.

The evidence given so far relates to the effect of certain job characteristics on worker *attitudes*. But the same characteristics were also responsible for certain kinds of overt behavior. Workers whose jobs had "high mass production scores" — that is, exhibited mass production characteristics in an extreme form — were absent more often from their jobs than workers on jobs with low mass production scores. More workers quit jobs with high mass production scores than quit jobs with low ones.

We believe it would be a mistake if the reader were to equate the workers' dislike of certain types of work with a dislike of work generally, including "hard work." This is a conclusion which certain commentators reach whenever it is reported that any group of industrial workers dislikes some element in their jobs. The Plant X workers were selected from a very large number of applicants on the basis of the character of their past records. When criticizing work at Plant X, they frequently added the assurance that they "could take it," or "it wasn't as bad as some people said," or they'd "get used to it," or "it was worth it because of the money and steady employment." But when all such reservations are made, the finding remains that a large majority of line workers voted immediate job content as their number one reason for *not* liking their jobs.

What can be done about this condition for the Plant X workers or for workers like them? The main answers to that question advanced in this inquiry are based on what the workers at Plant X did, said, or implied as to what they themselves would like. Many constructive ideas were offered. No one proposed the abolition of assembly lines or mass production methods — or capitalism. Their suggestions, direct or implied, were within the general framework of their own personal plant experience.

The mass production characteristic disliked most by a majority of workers in our sample was mechanical *pacing*. It is impossible

completely to separate pacing from repetitiveness either as regards these components in their own right or as regards workers'
suggestions about them. Nonetheless, so far as possible we shall
focus first on pacing.

Evidence for the dislike of this job component came in several
ways. It was number one on the rating scale as that part of the
immediate job most disliked. Other evidence came from rating of
the item "physically tiring" as number two in the dislike column.
Many explained that the job tired them out not because of muscular effort, but because of the tension and pace of the line. Reinforcing these ratings was a very large number of qualitative comments bluntly expressing a dislike of the conveyor which were
made without solicitation and not in answer to any specific question.

Of equal importance were indirect comments. A considerable
number of workers spoke of how much they liked their particular
work because it was *not* paced by the line. A repairman, quoted
earlier, gave a clear account of job components he liked, almost
all of which were the positive counterparts of those he did not.
His remarks started with pacing: "We don't feel the pressure of
the line since we don't have to do just one thing in a given area
and length of time." Then he said specifically that he liked his
job because he could set his own pace. Before the interview was
over, he had covered almost all characteristics of assembly work
which we have been studying by naming their opposites on the
rating scale: "Have interesting work, have to use my brains, do
different things, can talk with others, can work alone [this feature
more commonly occurred in dislike ratings], can move around
on the job," and "can choose how the job is to be done." As reasons for liking his job he put "can set my own pace" first, followed by "good working conditions" and "steady work."

Though we asked no direct attitude questions on this central
characteristic of an automobile assembly plant, pace and the
moving conveyor, nearly every worker expressed himself about
it at one time or another in the interview. These free association

comments demonstrated that (1) a large majority regarded the conveyor as an undesirable feature of the job, and (2) only a small minority were indifferent to or preferred the moving line.

What, then, were the suggestions, expressed or implied, for dealing with the pacing component of an assembly man's job?

The simplest and one of the commonest was for a rest period. Such an innovation would not, of course, vary the work pace while the line was in operation. Nor would it give the line worker any active control over his pace. It would, however, alter the total impact, both physical and psychological, of mechanical pacing on the individual by introducing a break. That break would presumably come at the time when monotony and tension were at their peak. As studies in other plants have shown, workers often remark that a rest period is "something to look forward to" and also that after it the work seems "lighter and easier."

A second recommendation implied by many comments was for more "banks." A worker who "builds a bank," the reader may remember, accumulates a visible pile or quantity of the product. Commonly in an auto assembly plant he builds up small sub-assemblies of door locks and handles, for example. From the worker's standpoint, the advantage is that he may — within limits — vary his work pace. Our interviews with "bank builders" showed a higher than average degree of job satisfaction. In the example given earlier of a worker who built up a pile of blower-defrosters, we commented that instead of the moving conveyor, the stock-chaser who brings him materials and takes away the finished assembly is his determinant of pace.

Besides the ability to vary pace, there is probably another basis for a bank builder's job satisfaction. That is the visible, tangible and controllable evidence of accomplishment as the bank which began at zero grows to appreciable size. Workers on many operations in other types of manufacture have given testimony on this point.

For the above reasons we believe the psychological satisfaction of bank building is worth further investigation and experiment.

Unfortunately, on the main line as it is presently laid out, a great deal of space is needed for a bank of chassis or bodies or completed cars. Therefore, the area offering the greatest possibility for experimentation would appear to lie in sub-assembly operations.

An actual change in pace was achieved by certain workers on the main line who were so situated that they could "work up the line" very fast and then briefly stop work altogether. By working very fast on say four or five units and then waiting for the conveyor to catch up with them, they could both vary their pace and "catch a spell." Line jobs where this was possible were preferred, but their number was limited. Working back is impossible when a man cannot start his operation until a preceding one is finished, when his tools are stationary, when he has several different operations to perform, or when the conveyor is speeded up.

The recommendation implied by many workers, then, is an increase in the number of jobs on which they can, within limits, vary their pace by working up the line. If such a practice is mentioned to a supervisor, he is apt to say, "The men aren't supposed to do it, but we wink at it." Why wink at it? Why not encourage the practice and so make it easier for more workers to vary their pace?

In fields of mechanical innovation it is common practice to conduct trial experiments. Similarly, if we were to set up an experimental unit — from the standpoint of a satisfactory adjustment of the pacing problem for the worker — it would include at least four elements: (1) a short line with rest periods and with collective pace control by the work group, (2) an interdependent functional relationship among members of the group, (3) bank building, and (4) a group incentive.

The above model is suggested not as an immediate and full answer to auto assembly problems, but as a suggested general approach to the problems of mechanical pacing. Coöperators in such an experiment should include supervisors, engineers, possibly a social scientist or two, and union representatives.

We turn now to the problem of how to introduce variety into a *repetitive* job. Notice that if the suggestions that follow were implemented, although directed mainly at repetitiveness, they would also to an important degree affect the pace of work.

With the exception of 10 per cent of our sample, variety was a valued component of the job. Evidence for this point, as we have seen, was direct and indirect: workers who had repetitive jobs said that they disliked them; workers whose jobs offered some degree of variety, especially the repair and utilitymen, praised that feature of their jobs. A correlation was found between verbal expressions of interest in work and the absolute number of operations performed on the job. As the number of operations increased, expressed interest in work increased; as they decreased, expressed interest in the work fell off.

From these facts, as well as from recommendations made by the workers themselves, two main suggestions emerge for increasing this variety component in assembly work. The first is job rotation, the second job enlargement.

In terms of the work experience of the utilitymen, job rotation is actually practiced at Plant X. The reader will remember that the utilityman in an automobile assembly plant is a relief worker who is competent to take over any job in his section for a longer or a shorter interval. The job satisfaction of the utilitymen as a group was high, and none complained of mechanical pacing or repetitiveness. According to their own testimony, their greater than average job satisfaction appeared to derive from their constant rotation among jobs. They spoke of an absence of monotony in their work, of getting an idea of the whole line (in their section), of meeting and talking with different workers as they were shifted about, and of having pride in knowing all the jobs. "In the battle of production," as one outside observer put it, "instead of being confined to a single fox-hole, they were able to swing their sights to include one whole platoon."

A basic point to notice is that this type of job rotation, which clearly means job enrichment for the individual, does no violence to basic mass production principles. The engineer has broken the assembly process at any given point into simple constituent operations geared to certain mechanical imperatives of the machinery. These operations have been further analyzed into simple sets of bodily motions to be made by each worker. If the engineer has done his job properly, the motions are the most convenient and economical possible. This practice of job analysis, which is basic to mass production, clearly remains in force when a utilityman replaces say a grinder at his regular job. It remains in force when a utilityman performs half a dozen different jobs in one day on the line. From an engineering standpoint, each job he performs has been developed from the analysis of the requisite simple constituent motions. *But from the standpoint of the utilityman, his work experience for that day has been quite different from the work experience of any one of the job holders whom he replaced.* This point is worth special emphasis because it removes a common misconception. Many persons in and out of industry believe that variety cannot be reintroduced into the modern industrial plant without abandoning the basic principles of progressive manufacture. This is clearly untrue.

The utilityman is not, to be sure, a craftsman in the traditional sense. The work he performs, when subdivided into sufficiently short time cycles, is strictly paced, repetitive, and routine. When he has mastered say twenty of these jobs, however, *he becomes* in a very real sense *a skilled workman.* It is also important to emphasize that more than a merely additive process has taken place. For the utilitymen with whom we talked an integrative process had occurred in the course of the learning and the doing of many jobs. These men now understood the total production job for a given segment of the line, say the assembly of seat springs or the installation of motors. And with that integration came satisfaction and often pride in the *whole* product.

The next step in this chain of reasoning is obvious. If the utilityman can perform several jobs, in each of them keeping up with the line, and derive substantial satisfaction from his multiple task, why can't the average worker? We believe that in a great many work situations he can and would prefer to do so. Here is part of the evidence. At Plant X we were struck with the unusually high degree of job satisfaction expressed by the members of one work group under a particular foreman. With the permission and encouragment of their foreman, the men were working under a system of job rotation. It was to this system that the members of the group ascribed their relatively high job satisfaction. And to the same system the section foreman owed in part a smoothly running and efficient work unit. Top plant management is now encouraging a more widespread application of this practice.

In connection with any system of job rotation certain questions come immediately to mind:

(1) Since it requires some effort to learn several jobs instead of one, will the worker, unless he is exceptional, object? Managers who have difficulty in getting workers to change jobs frequently say "yes."

(2) Will the rotated worker do his jobs as fast or as well as the stationary worker?

The obvious answer to the first question about worker resistance to rotation is the pragmatic one. In certain sections on the line at Plant X rotation is working. In other industries and on other types of assembly lines the practice of rotation is steadily gaining ground.* For most people, learning to do something new is hard work, and it is only undertaken when an adequate reward is held out. For a considerable number of assembly line workers the rewards of variety and of possessing a repertory of skills will be sufficient. But on the other hand, some resistance to an experiment in rotation is to be expected. The key to the

---

* Example of successful application of the principle of job rotation among repetitive jobs is afforded by the Bristol-Myer Company at their Hillside, New Jersey, plant. Operators learn jobs in blocs of twelve and receive an increase in pay on successfully mastering each new bloc. Management reports that job rotation has proved more efficient than individual job assignment.

situation lies, we suggest, in the word "experiment." Where rotation has been successfully installed on other types of assembly lines, it has usually been started as an experiment, with management guaranteeing to the work group or to any single individual a return to stationary assignments if desired, and rarely have the workers wished to return.

What about the second question: will the work be done as well or as fast under job rotation? The answer for the Plant X section practicing it was affirmative. For other work groups in other industries with which the authors are familiar, the answer has also been "yes." Of course, there are work situations where job rotation appears either altogether impractical or less efficient. But is the over-all and long term performance of the group necessarily less efficient? Gains in quality and a drop in turnover or absenteeism may balance some decrease in output, if it occurs.

Job enlargement is the second recommendation that emerged in our study of repetitiveness. It is a concept and a practice that has proved successful in decreasing monotony without impairing efficiency in certain sectors of other industries. We here suggest that it be introduced experimentally into auto assembly work. Job enlargement is simply the recombining of two or more separate jobs into one. Certain plant managers in other industries have been finding that a law of diminishing returns applies to the subdivision of jobs and that a recombination of certain fractured parts has increased efficiency.* This means a lengthening of time cycles. Job enlargement in the sense in which we suggest it does not mean turning automobile assembly back into the hands of master mechanics with one worker assigned to the assembly of one car. It does mean that greater attention be paid to psychological and social variables in the determination of time cycles, and, by the same token, more attention be paid to the *content* of individual jobs.

To one unfamiliar with assembly line work experience, the

---

* Charles R. Walker, "The Problem of the Repetitive Job," *Harvard Business Review*, vol. XXVIII, no. 3 (May, 1950), p. 54.

difference between a job with five operations and a job with ten, or between a job taking two minutes to perform and a job taking four might seem a matter far too trivial to concern anyone. Our data have shown that this is not true. Management has a vital interest in such matters: the proper assignment of time cycles throughout an assembly plant will make an important difference in the efficiency of the plant. As for the worker, one of the most striking findings of this study is the psychological importance of even minute changes in his immediate job experience. The point may be given an oversimplified summary by saying: other things being equal, the difference between a satisfied and a dissatisfied worker *may* rest on whether he has a five-operation or a ten-operation job.

A majority of the workers' suggestions for improving their jobs were tied to pace and repetitiveness, the first two components on our list. What about the others? As we turn to these other characteristics of assembly line work, it will become apparent that any change in the first two is likely to affect one or more of the others.

Minimum skill. Out of our analysis of skills or the lack of them in assembly line work, two or three points stand out. No adequate method of classifying and evaluating skills had been applied in Plant X. The general public and even some members of management tended to depreciate the amount and variety of skills required. An unfortunate social and psychological corollary was that workers tended to devaluate themselves and to exhibit symptoms of inferiority when discussing the skill component of their jobs. This reaction was probably more pronounced among Plant X workers, who were recruited from non-mass production jobs, than it would have been in an area where the population had become culturally conditioned to such jobs.

Possibly something can be done about this by management apart from changing job content. But more important, if the recommendations just made for increasing variety were carried out, obviously the component of skill on the job would also be considerably increased. And if the experience of other companies is any criterion, added increments of skill, apart from more basic satisfactions, will add prestige value to the average job.

All mass production jobs in modern industry, but especially the jobs of an automobile assembly line, are strictly *predetermined as to tools and techniques.* Many men indicated that they would have liked some freedom in planning their work and in the use of tools. But here is a component which is quite unaffected however much you enlarge or rotate assembly line jobs. The same moving conveyor will move at the same pace, the same electric drills, air screw drivers, polishing wheels, and so forth, will be essential for the job. In spite of the apparently immutable character of this component, however, we suggest that it presents a challenging field for experimentation. For example, once a year at the time of model changes there is a period when tools and methods are changed, and when the whole process and organization are fluid. It is worth considering whether or not this period might offer a time for greater participation by the workers in the setting up of their jobs for the rest of the year. In other industries the increased participation by workers in the methods and scheduling of work has proved a source of both job satisfaction and greater efficiency.

Peter Drucker discusses this point and suggests in effect that predetermination of tools and techniques has gone too far when it completely precludes any participation by workers in organizing their own jobs.*

The industrial engineer sees in the human being a tool and that means that, to him, the human being is the more productive, the more thoroughly his work has been set up and laid out **for** him.

The social scientist lays stress on man's need to participate. He, therefore, concludes that the human being is the more productive

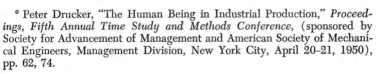

* Peter Drucker, "The Human Being in Industrial Production," *Proceedings, Fifth Annual Time Study and Methods Conference,* (sponsored by Society for Advancement of Management and American Society of Mechanical Engineers, Management Division, New York City, April 20–21, 1950), pp. 62, 74.

and the more efficient, the more **he himself** designs and lays out his own work.

The solution of this conflict seems to me to lie in the approach to the problem of the individual and the group . . .

It would seem to follow . . . that the spot to apply scientific management is not perhaps the work of the individual but the work of the group. It would also follow that the place where the individual should be given and can be given participation in the decisions regarding his own work is the group. The work of the group, in other words, should be set up by scientific management and on industrial engineering standards. **But within the group there should be considerable latitude to enable the members to organize the work their own way."** (Boldface added.)

Minute division of product. We quoted earlier a Plant X worker who said, "I'd like to do a whole fender myself from the raw material to the finished job. It would be more interesting." It is unlikely that this worker will ever get his wish. However, he would have an approximation and perhaps a psychological equivalent if the recommendations made for enlarging or rotating jobs were implemented. Even apart from those recommendations, there are certain practices in other industries and possibly in other parts of the automobile industry which might help. For operators working on minute parts of the end product, it has become standard practice in some shops to give demonstrations of the role of that particular part in the functioning of the final product. A familiar example is showing war workers how a single badly manufactured piece will put a gun out of commission. The psychological importance of tying your own particular work, however fractional, to the final product, when that product is sufficiently interesting or socially important, is well illustrated by a Plant X worker whose job was near the end of the final line:

If they rush us, we can't get too good quality. You scratch the panels and so forth. We used to be too rushed, but now we have rearranged the job and get along pretty well. I get along with

* *Ibid.*, p. 71.

the fellows and **get some satisfaction out of the job.** When I walk to the end of the line and see the finished car, it makes me feel good, knowing I helped make it. I always wonder who will get the finished car I see.

Surface mental attention. The mental demands of a majority of automobile assembly jobs are for surface attention. Workers must give a high degree of attention to their work, they cannot daydream; yet the work does not absorb their mental faculties to any depth.

This kind of intermediate category — between the automatic "do it without thinking" job and the mentally absorbing job — is the type most conducive to boredom. We recommend, therefore, that assembly line jobs be studied from this standpoint and either be more fully mechanized if possible, that is, made more automatic, or be enlarged and made more absorbing by a process of recombination. The principle here is a simple one. It is desirable that modern technology either release the mind for other activity or be such as to absorb and make some use of the mental faculties of human beings.

In addition, even with all the mechanical improvements of the past twenty years, there is still considerable physical drudgery on assembly lines. Further mechanization is urged to lift this load from the muscles of the assembly man.

All of the characteristics or components of the assembly man's immediate job we have just reviewed were found to have a bearing upon the quality of the product. Although restricting it, mass production methods did not eliminate the "human factor" as a determinant of quality for any given part or for the total product. Most workers were found to be conscious of this factor. For a substantial number inability to put out quality was a source of irritation, putting out quality a source of job satisfaction.

IMPACT OF MASS PRODUCTION CHARAC-
TERISTICS ON SOCIAL STRUCTURE

Mass production methods clearly impinge on the worker in two ways, directly through the immediate content of his daily work indirectly by molding and modifying the social structure of in-plant society in which he spends his working hours. This indirect impact on the individual, though not as obvious as the direct effect of a moving conveyor on the muscles of a worker who has to keep up with it, appears to be of equal importance in conditioning job satisfaction.

As applied on an automobile assembly line, mass production technology and its methods affect various aspects of social organization in the factory, but chiefly these:

(1) The size and function of work groups.

(2) The quality and quantity of interaction possible among workers.

(3) Functional relations between supervisor and worker and the kind of informal social interaction between them.

(4) The wage structure.

(5) The character of the system of promotion and transfer. These several effects also appear to condition the role which the union plays for the average assembly worker.

The first two points, determination of groups and conditioning of interaction among workers, were discussed mainly in Chapter V. The automobile assembly process as organized today imposes a loose work group whose members are related to each other through proximity and not through mutual assistance; most workers, especially those on the line, are in this category. It also creates a few isolates, who enjoy no social interaction during their working hours, and a few groups whose members are functionally knit in a true team relationship.

One of the interesting results of our study, therefore, is a fairly clear picture of the *kind* of social interaction a moving belt technology permits and also of the kind it denies. Most commonly it permits, as indicated, a loose work group of five or six operators who can make brief remarks to one another during the working day. Each individual is part of a group with a slightly different membership from the group of every other operator, because each successive operator along the line loses one member on one side as he gains one on the other. It denies to all but a few operators a functional or team relationship with other workers. Ability to interact is also heavily conditioned on some jobs by such factors as noise, speed of the line, and the amount of physical energy demanded.

Since the character of social relationships in an assembly plant is thus closely linked with process, technology, and layout, it is suggested that the engineering department restudy jobs and layout with these factors in mind. Especially when modifications in process and layout normally occur, it may be possible to increase the quota of workers who are on teams and reduce the number of those experiencing less satisfying work relationships. Or where this is not possible, there may be an opportunity to increase the number of social contacts through job rotation. Finally, realization of its importance may bring about the reduction of noise and of other factors making social interaction difficult or impossible.

Present and previous studies made by the authors suggest that technological factors have a profound effect in determining the kind of relations which the worker experiences with all ranks of supervision. A useful way of describing and of measuring these relations is by reporting the quantity and quality of social interaction.

In Chapter VII, "The Worker and Supervision," we showed that the interaction rate was exceptionally low between workers and all ranks of supervision except section foremen. This situation in Plant X was in sharp contrast to the close-knit relationship and high rate of interaction in some basic industries with which the authors are familiar. We illustrated these sharp contrasts between Plant X and a steel mill. The frequency rate of interaction between the worker and his immediate foreman was high —

several times a day — in both auto and steel plants. But above the rank of section foreman, the workers in the steel mill had contact with their supervisors, general foremen, assistant superintendent, and superintendent (of the department) five to ten times as often as did the workers in the auto plant. Some of the latter had neither met nor knew the name of their general foremen, or of the supervisors above them.

The basic factor which appeared to determine the rate and quality of worker-supervisor interaction was technology. The production process in steel making required frequent interaction between workers and everyone up to and including department superintendents. Supervisors in auto assembly, on the other hand, except at the section level, could carry out their duties impersonally and with little or no contact with the workers.

It would seem reasonable, then, to ascribe partially to this condition the sense of impersonality so often mentioned by production workers at Plant X, as well as the fact that a substantial number of workers did not identify themselves favorably with the company or the corporation.

What might be done to alter this situation? Although the basis for the contrast under discussion appears to be clearly technological, we believe that management has some power to modify within limits the existing worker-supervisor relationship in the direction of greater social interaction. In this instance both Plant X and Corporation X management have agreed. If, however, the quantity of such interaction between workers and upper supervision were increased, what would be its content? If upper supervision were simply told to talk to production workers more than they had been doing, little or nothing of value would result, we believe, from such artificial stimulation. If, on the other hand, before initiating such a policy it were recognized by both groups that they had much of mutual interest to tell each other about the assembly of automobiles and about Plant X as a production team, something of great value to human relations might accrue.

The other two areas in which we found that mass production

technology affected social organization were the wage structure and the system of promotion and transfer. Both may be considered together because both *effects* flow from the same mass production principle.

Through extreme fractionalizing of the process and its reduction to simple constituent motions, jobs as well as parts have become standardized and, like the parts, to a considerable extent interchangeable. We have spent a good deal of time in attempting to show that the jobs really are not all alike by pointing out all the minute differences. We are not now reversing ourselves. Those minute differences are of great importance to the mind and muscles of the individual worker day by day. But from management's point of view, the jobs are much the same. Nearly every worker could learn nearly every job in a relatively short time, if necessary. And for this reason management feels justified in paying roughly the same to everybody. As we pointed out in our discussion of pay and security, Chapter VI, three-fourths of the one thousand production workers in Plant X fall into only four job classifications. In our sample the spread between the lowest and the highest paid production worker was only twelve cents. This is what we mean when we say that mass production methods have affected the wage structure. They have affected it by standardizing wages to accord with standardized jobs and by narrowing the span between the lowest and highest paid job. As we pointed out once before, it is incorrect to attribute all of this standardization to mass production principles. The union has reinforced the same tendency toward leveling of wages by raising lower paid workers and leaving the higher categories alone.*

By the same token, both of these forces, the mass production tendency toward simplifying and standardizing jobs and union pressure for wage equalization, have given the auto assembly plants of the country the kind of promotion system they have.

---

* It is interesting to note that just in the past year the UAW-CIO itself did something to reverse this trend by again bargaining strongly on behalf of skilled workers.

That is a system with a very short progression ladder. Roughly speaking, the production worker is on a floor or a gently sloping ramp, not a ladder. Hence, when he really thinks about promotion, he has to think not about regular job progression up the visible and recognized steps of a job ladder, but rather of getting onto the next floor by becoming a foreman or a utilityman, for example, or else of moving laterally into another department altogether to become a maintenance man or a stock clerk.

This is one of the most important effects of mass production methods on industrial organization. By all but obliterating job progression among production workers, it strikes at one of the strongest human incentives. It also strikes at a cultural tradition closely interwoven with American ideas and ideals — the belief in the desirability and possibility of "rising in the world." The immediate world of the auto assembler is the factory. It is still possible to rise in that world and even out of it, but each year it is becoming more difficult.

We have been saying that mass production methods touch the social structure or social organization of the plant at five points. It is interesting and important to notice that at each one of these points the effect on the individual who lives within that social structure is the same. The effect is one of *de*-personalization or, put in another way, of increasing the individual worker's sense of anonymity within the general mass of his fellow workers.

To illustrate, in so far as the technology of the line keeps the work groups weak and nonfunctional, it tends by that much to weaken the individual's sense of belonging to a bona fide industrial community. There is a close personal work bond between the individual and his immediate boss, but all other bonds either with supervision or with local management are non-personal or impersonal. Again, at the end of every two-week period when the worker receives his pay envelope, the wages inside it will be roughly of the same amount as the wages of hundreds of others. Every job on the line is slightly different from every other — and these differences he appreciates keenly, but there is only a slight difference in what one pays as against another, together with little if any difference in status or prestige.

Therefore, any production worker can, and sometimes does, say: "There are hundreds of jobs like mine, not much better, not much worse. The differences are so slight, or seem so slight to management, that I am interchangeable." To escape this impersonality quite as much, perhaps, as to escape monotony, the average worker does not aspire to climb into another slightly better production job, but into a utilityman's or a repairman's where he can be recognized and where also he can recognize himself as an individual.

We suggest that the sense of becoming *de*-personalized, of becoming anonymous as against remaining one's self, is for those who feel it a psychologically more disturbing result of the work environment than either the boredom or the tension that arise from repetitive and mechanically paced work. This appeared to be the basis of such bitterly critical comments as were made against Company X as such. If we are to "do something about" depersonalization, the first step is to understand it. Here we suggest the hypothesis that basically it stems not directly from mass production methods and principles, but indirectly from their impact — in such ways as we have reviewed above — on the social structure of in-plant society.

Some if not all of the effects we reviewed have determined in part perhaps the particular role which the union plays for the Plant X work force. The evidence of qualitative remarks suggests that the local tends to fill a social need resulting from the impersonal relations within the plant. The chief determinant of this situation would appear to be a technological one. Apart from its usual function as bargaining agent, qualitative comments suggests also that the union tends to modify for the average worker the sense of anonymity and of depersonalization which he receives during his hours of work in the plant.

THE PROBLEM IN PERSPECTIVE

Throughout this study both union and management agreed with the authors that the basic problems to be explored were not those connected with a particular plant, industry, or corporation. Rather they were problems related to basic technological and organizational trends in modern industry. Both agreed that modern American civilization as we know it rests upon mass production principles quite as much as upon the natural resources of the United States. The attitude of both, therefore, was a simple one: *Since these problems exist, let us get all the facts we can. In time we shall be able to solve them.*

Up to 1914, modern industrialism as a fully accepted way of life prevailed chiefly in England, North America, and certain countries of Western Europe, particularly, of course, Germany. South America generally, the Balkan countries, the Near and the Far East — Japan excepted — and Africa were still outside the orbit or circle of full industrialization. Since 1914 everything has changed. The most important event of the present half century from the standpoint of culture in the anthropological sense has been large-scale industrialization within the vast Eurasian land mass under Russian rule.

As a result of this, and as a result of the rapid development and spread of mass production methods during these years in Europe, but especially in the United States, we now stand on the threshold of a new movement for the diffusion of industrialism throughout the habitable world. Obviously, the possibilities for improvement of the health and well being of the population of the world are immense. Also the possibility of avoiding some of mankind's earlier mistakes associated with the first industrial revolution is not to be overlooked.

In the interest of defense we are today exporting to Europe not only a great volume of material goods, including machinery for both peace and war, but more important, actual blueprints as well as knowledge of the principles and practice of mass production. For four years the Marshall Plan has been the symbol of such export. But Russia, too, is exporting industrial techniques both to her satellite countries and to the Far East, together with her own version of how they should be administered.

In this general diffusion of the techniques and know-how of mass production, the countries and peoples who adopt them may make all of our mistakes and the mistakes of our forefathers who introduced to a complacent century the tragic years of the first industrial revolution. They may even add a few new mistakes of their own for good measure. But it is also possible that mankind is being offered a kind of second chance in adapting the machine to human ends. There is at least one basis for such a hope — the young but rapidly growing science of Man as it is branching forth into such subjects as industrial psychology and sociology, and cultural anthropology, together with the science, and art, of human relations in industry. In any case, it seems a peculiarly appropriate time to accelerate the social study of mass production techniques, the most famous of all commodities made in the United States, and now clearly marked for export to the rest of the world.

METHOD OF RESEARCH

In planning the present study, careful consideration was given to the following problems:

I. How to gain the coöperation of all parties concerned.

II. How to arrive at a representative sample.

III. How to construct a reliable questionnaire which would give valid results.

In the discussion below these three points are developed.

I. COÖPERATION OF PARTIES CONCERNED

A. MANAGEMENT

Early in 1949, after a series of conferences with top company management, the authors received permission to proceed with a study of production workers in one of the company's plants, which is designated as Plant X. Further conferences were then arranged with local plant managerial representatives. In making this request, it was understood that all names would be treated in confidence; in other words, that neither management nor, in fact, anyone else was to know who was to be selected for interview. Likewise, the details of the questionnaire were shown to no one.

An important object in these early conferences with local management was to make sure that the managerial staff, and especially lower supervision, had no misunderstanding regarding the auspices, the scope, and the purpose of our research. It was made clear (1) that this study was being carried out by Yale University, (2) that it was being done as a public service, (3) that it would be centered upon assembly line workers, and (4) that it was intended to increase our knowledge of human behavior in industry under certain technological conditions. The research, it was pointed out, was not concerned with the competence or personality of individual employees, whether supervisors or workers.

B. THE UNION

We informed the international union of our intention and purposes and then held a conference with the local officers and a staff representative of the international. It was again explained that the study was to be conducted by Yale University as a public service, that the workers would be interviewed in their homes (and only if they wished), and finally, that in publishing the results of our study, no individual or group would be identified. After checking with the international officers, the president of the local reported that the union had no objection to the study's being made.

C. THE COMMUNITY

It was decided that our object would be served best if we avoided publicity in the communities where the workers lived. The only contact made with any community official was at the beginning of the study when we sought the aid of the executive secretary of the Chamber of Commerce in Town X to procure maps and find an office for project headquarters. Our program was stated in general terms to the secretary. We requested that no publicity be given to the project and that should he hear of criticism, he notify the research staff immediately. At no time during the three months when interviews took place were comments of any kind brought to our attention. At the end of the field research period, the Chamber of Commere official said that he had heard no criticism.

In other communities our policy was to contact only the workers whom we were interested in interviewing. In our talks with them we found no indication that townspeople took any active interest in either promoting or hindering our program.

Throughout the period of study we had no evidence that any members of either management, the union, or the community had attempted to influence the replies given by the workers to our questions. In a few instances, workers checked with the local union president to verify the purposes and auspices of the project before agreeing upon a time for an interview.

D. THE RESEARCH PERSONNEL

A brief word might be said regarding the selection of interviewers. We sought persons with some background in the study of human relations in industry and with some knowledge of research techniques. After screening a number of applicants, three men were chosen. All three were matriculated Ph.D. candidates from the Department of Industrial Relations at Massachusetts Institute of Technology.

During the early phases of field research, our plans and policies were carefully outlined to the interviewers. When the preliminary interviewing program began, daily staff conferences were held. Problems were fully explored and discussed. Interview questions were added, revised, or eliminated. Care was exercised to see to it that everyone fully understood precisely what was intended by each question.

When the full interviewing program got under way, a member of the staff remained "on location" to make appointments, advise the interviewers, and check their completed questionnaires following the interviews.

E. THE WORKERS

One of the first and most basic decisions in planning the present project was to interview workers in their homes. Our reasoning was simple. We rejected the idea of interviewing in the plant, at the union offices, or in any location which might be construed to mean that we were representing some organization other than Yale University.

Workers were first approached by telephone. In making the introductory call, a member of the staff explained who he was and what the purpose of the study was. Generally, the points made in this introduction included the following statements: (1) Yale University is making studies of jobs in various industries. (2) This year a study is being carried on among automobile assembly line workers at Plant X. (3) The names of several workers have been drawn anonymously from personnel records at Plant X. Neither the company nor anyone else knows the names of those chosen to be interviewed. (4) The information given by the worker will be treated in confidence and no names used in the published study.

Following the telephone discussion, an appointment was made for an interview. At the designated time an interviewer called at the man's house and made himself known. Each carried a letter of identification, but it was seldom requested.

The interview was usually preceded by a few minutes of general conversation,* after which the interviewer began to ask questions regarding the worker's past employment history. After some experimenta-

---

* We soon found that a prerequisite for a successful interview was a thorough knowledge on the part of the interviewer of the winnings, losings, line-ups, and batting averages of the workers' favorite baseball teams.

tion, this appeared to be the most natural kind of approach leading to a discussion of the present job.

Notes were made by the interviewer as the worker spoke, and each evening following the interviews the notes were transcribed in full. A rule was made that only the workers' *own* words were to be recorded. No interpolations by the interviewer were permitted. Space was left at the end of the questionnaire for any comments the interviewers thought would be enlightening in data analysis.

Care was taken by the interviewers to lead the worker as naturally as possible from one question to another. If a worker chose to dwell on a particular subject, he was not interrupted. If he wished to jump to questions taken up in other parts of the questionnaire, that too was permitted. In short, every effort was made to keep as many attributes of a free-association interview as possible within the framework of a more formal schedule.

At the close of each interview, the respondent was again assured that nothing he had said would be repeated to others.

II. THE SAMPLE

In June, 1949, there were approximately 1,800 wage and salaried persons working at Plant X. Of this number, 1,386 were hourly paid employees in the production and non-production departments.* Among the group of 1,386 men, 1,068 were production workers. The remaining 318 were maintenance, janitorial, stock jig and fixture, inspection, and miscellaneous hourly paid personnel. Our interest centered on the 1,068 production workers.

Although there were seventy-seven job classifications covering these production workers, it was found that 80 per cent were in fourteen different job classes. The number in each of the fourteen classes ranged from fifteen to 249 men. Because these classes represented the whole range of "typical" assembly operations, it was decided to draw the sample from the 848 men in these classes.

Of the 848 workers in this group, 146 were newcomers who had been employed less than six months. By eliminating these, the potential sample was reduced to 702.

The next sampling problem was that of residence location. Workers at Plant X came from 102 different towns and cities within a radius

---

* The remaining group of approximately 400 employees were managers, supervisors, engineers, office clericals, and office personnel of the various staff and service departments.

of thirty-five miles. It was considered impractical to extend the sample geographically to include all locations. Therefore, towns in which less than ten workers lived were eliminated. Nevertheless, the number of workers living at different distances from the town in which Plant X was located was proportionately represented in our final sample.

The potential sample was 414 after we had eliminated workers for the reasons stated above. Of this number another forty-two were dropped for miscellaneous reasons. Three had left the company between June and the time of the interview. A small number was eliminated because no telephone numbers were available. There was nothing to indicate that this group of forty-two might have biased the sample by their absence.

The "working potential" of the study thus became 372 men comprising 44 per cent of the 848 workers in the selected job classifications, or 53 per cent of those in the job classifications who had been employed at Plant X for at least six months. Of the 372 workers, a stratified group of 180 was interviewed.

The men were stratified according to job classification, department, age, education, marital status, dwelling status, and veteran status. By so doing, we gained a proportional representation of the total 848 in terms of these categories. In no category did the number in our sample vary from the sample category in the total population by more than 6 per cent. In most instances it was less than 3 per cent.

Having assured ourselves of the adequacy of the sample in terms of proportion and stratification "fit," there remained the possibility of bias due to actual interview refusals. A careful record was made of all telephone calls and personal contacts with workers. There were many instances when interviews could not be arranged for a number of reasons. But in only five instances did workers refuse to make an appointment. In all other cases reasonable excuses were given, and in almost all of these cases the workers voluntarily suggested some specific time for the interview to take place in the future.

What about cases when the interviewers were "stood up" once appointments were made? Here, too, the record was good. In five instances there were unexplained absences from the interview. In thirty-five instances the interview "fell through" but a recheck proved that the excuse was valid. Usually a man's absence was due to unpredicted overtime work. In most instances the worker suggested that another date be set.

III. THE QUESTIONNAIRE

The data recorded upon the final interview schedules consisted of (a) factual statements and (b) attitudes and opinions.

Certain factual data were immediately transcribed from the personnel records of Plant X to the interview sheets. This included the worker's name, address, telephone number, age, education, veteran status, marital and dwelling status, job classification, previous employment, and so forth.

Additional factual material came from direct questioning of the workers. This included information as to the number of men in a work group, interaction with fellow workers and supervision, number and kinds of jobs worked on in Plant X, number of union meetings attended, and so forth. Further factual information was drawn from workers' descriptions of present and previous jobs. In a discussion of jobs held prior to coming to Plant X, the general question was asked: "Just what did you do on that job?" From the relatively extensive answers given by the workers, we were able to record the type of industry, occupation, and skill. We then determined whether or not the pace at which a man had worked had been controlled by a prescribed schedule, by mechanical means, by the man himself, or by some other factor. This previous job data supplied by the workers also indicated whether or not their motions had been repetitive, what types of tools and materials they used, and whether they had worked on the whole, a substantial part, or merely a minute fraction of the product or service, and many other work characteristics.

There were a few questions which might be called quasi-factual, where the response was actually only an opinion about a fact. For example, workers were asked how long it took them to learn their present jobs well enough to keep up with their fellow workers. A man's answer might be a fact or what he supposed to be a fact. In the analysis such quasi-factual data was recognized as such. On the particular question of learning time we found that the responses generally agreed with management estimates.

The majority of interview questions were designed not to elicit facts but to draw out workers' attitudes and opinions. For such questions we used a variety of forms including the simple yes-no and the multiple choice types of question. "Do you think you are doing the job that suits you best at Plant X" is an example of the simple "yes-no" or "don't know" question. The respondent in all cases, however, was asked to explain and amplify what lay back of his positive or negative answer.

The multiple choice type of question allowed for a range of answers between extremes, and was based upon answers received in our preliminary "feeler" interviews. In asking some questions, this range was spelled out for the respondent by the interviewer. In others, the interviewer simply asked the question and marked the interview sheet at the appropriate point in the range. Here is an example of the first type of question: when workers discussed present jobs they were asked, "As jobs at Plant X go, would you say you had one of the best, better than most, about average, not as good as most, or one of the poorest jobs?" The answer here was purposely limited to one of these five choices. Qualitative explanations given were also recorded.

An example of the second type of multiple choice question is: after naming the job he hoped to have some day, the worker was asked, "What do you think your chances are of getting that job?" The interviewer then checked one of the five kinds of answers which ranged from "good chance" to "poor chance." The worker's explanation was also recorded.

For a number of questions the open-ended technique was used, especially when the question might evoke a strong emotional response. Here we were anxious to avoid suggesting any arbitrary range of answers. For example, "What does your wife think about your job?" Whatever the worker replied the interviewer recorded exactly. Analysis and classification of such material was done after all the interviews had been completed. As a rule, it was possible to discriminate a range between extremes, as for example, from "generally favorable" to "generally unfavorable." A simple illustration of how such material was evaluated may be taken from responses to the wife-opinion question. A worker might answer, as many did, "She's glad I have a good paying job and steady work." If, after examining the total interview, there were no indications that the wife held adverse opinions, this answer was presumed to be generally favorable. On the other hand, such an answer as, "My wife doesn't like my job; she thinks I'm working too hard for my health," would be classified as unfavorable if there were no other indications in the interview to alter such a classification. If a worker were to say, "My wife likes the steady work and the good pay, but she says the grind is too much and that I ought to be in a job where I could work at my trade," the response would be classified as mixed favorable-unfavorable.

During the course of preliminary interviews, we began to accumulate reasons why the workers either liked or did not like their previous and present jobs. From these we constructed a two-column rating scale. In one column were listed the actual words and phrases most often used by workers to describe features they liked about their jobs. In the second column were listed the disliked features. The dislikes were often the opposites or counterparts of the features in the like column.

In the course of the interview the worker was asked to check the likes and dislikes for both his previous job and his present one at Plant X. He was also told that he could add any other features he wished. After he had checked all his likes and dislikes, he was then asked to take the lists and rate the three major likes and the three major dislikes in the order of their importance to him. As a rule, each step in this process was explained separately so that he could understand what he was doing and concentrate on one choice at a time. He was first asked to "pick out of all those things you like the one most important to you"; then, "now pick out the next in importance"; and finally, "now pick out the next."

These check lists have proved of great value in assisting the authors in the task of weighting job elements. They have been used throughout the study to show the relative importance in the total job situation of the several job factors which are treated in separate chapters.

One other technique was used in the interview. In discussing a worker's job on the assembly line, the interviewer sat down with the respondent and, with his assistance, carefully sketched on a sheet of paper the "geography" of the man's job. That is to say, the flow of work on the line, or off the line, was sketched out, and the worker's position was indicated in relation to work flow and to the group of men with whom he worked. Arrows of varying thickness were drawn to indicate the amount of social interaction taking place between the respondent and his fellow workers. This device gave a clearer picture of (a) the work flow, (b) the spatial relationship in the work environment, and (c) the social interaction pattern with reference to that environment.

BASIC CHARACTERISTICS OF THE WORKING FORCE AT PLANT X

AGE

Soon after this study began it became apparent that the work force of the new plant had one characteristic not typical of the industry or of manufacturing in general. That characteristic was youth. The average age of workers was twenty-seven. Among our sample of production workers only twenty (9 per cent) were over forty years old, while 114 (63.3 per cent) were thirty or under.

This heavy weighting in the direction of youth is not explained by chance. It is the result of a clear-cut policy on the part of the company to hire men in the younger age groups. The nature of many jobs requiring hard physical work necessitated the choice of younger men. Further, the plant was new. Personnel policy makers within the company wished to build up a core of men, many of whom might be expected to "grow up" with the plant. It was pointed out that other automotive assembly plants had in the past recruited young men at the start of operations.

Whatever the reasons for the company's accent on youth, the fact is obviously important to this study. The degree to which a worker adjusted to his new technological environment, his feelings toward his immediate job, his attitudes toward supervision and the company were presumably influenced to some degree by the age group to which he belonged. For example, we found a tendency for those who were old enough to have experienced the depression as unemployed adults to hold more favorable job attitudes than did the youngest group.

VETERAN STATUS

As might be expected from the age range of the group of workers, many were veterans of World War II. In fact, only 25.9 per cent were non-veterans.

While this study is not concerned with the impact of war service on job adjustment, it quickly became clear that a man's wartime experience had a bearing on job behavior. For persons in any occupation it might be expected that military experience would create occupational problems. One would suppose also that the problems would be more acute or at least different from the problems of those who had not undergone such an experience. Our evidence has suggested that work "on the line" did not provide the workers with the kind of "release from discipline" which they had hoped for in a civilian job. Often a man being interviewed would speak of the time when he would be "setting up [his] own little business." Conversely, when speaking about the assembly line, many of the veterans made comparisons with their military experience. However, instead of comparing discipline of military superiors to discipline of their occupational supervisors, they compared it with the discipline of the moving belt — the compulsion of the machine.

MARITAL STATUS

In considering the many factors influencing job adjustment to assembly line work, it seemed reasonable to suppose that marital status might be important. Among the group of 180 production workers, forty-five men were single, 133 were married, and two divorced or separated. This is a ratio of one single to three married men.

Our interest in recording information on marital status was centered on the question: "Do single men differ in the degree of job adjustment to assembly line work from men who bear the responsibility of a family?" The most that may be said from our available evidence is that married men at Plant X appeared to place a somewhat greater emphasis on pay and security than did single men.

DWELLING STATUS

As with marital and dependency status, it was thought that owning or not owning one's home might be expected to have some bearing on a man's occupational adjustment.

Among the group studied, it was found that 36.1 per cent rented their homes, 36.7 per cent lived with parents or relatives, 20.5 per cent owned or were buying their own homes, and 7.7 per cent were boarders.*

The high percentage of those renting or living with parents or relatives is explained both by the youth of the "population" and by the housing shortage current at the time. When married workers discussed

* In actual numbers, 65, 64, 37, and 14, respectively.

reasons why they liked working at Plant X, they frequently stated that it gave them the opportunity to plan for home ownership. This, in turn, often explained why some men continued to work at Plant X in spite of strong feelings against assembly line work.

EDUCATION

The objective requirements of a man's job are obviously often related to his educational qualifications. Again, job adjustment and satisfaction may be related to a person's level of schooling. Most jobs on the assembly line actually required little formal education or previous training. The average worker did not have to use "figures," for example, nor was there much need for speaking, reading, or writing ability.

TABLE **14**

Number of Grades of School Attended by Production Workers at Plant X [a]

Years of Schooling	Number of Men	Percentage
Less than 8	16	8.8
8	17	9.4
9–12	58	32.2
12	79	43.8
More than 12	10	5.5

[a] Does not include additional trade school education after regular schooling. Sample of 180 production workers.

In view of this condition, one might expect to find an average or perhaps below average level of formal education among the workers at Plant X. Such was not the case. As shown in Table 14, 81 per cent of the men had attended high school; 49 per cent of the entire sample were high-school graduates or higher. Only 8.8 per cent had less than eight-grade schooling. This may in part be explained by the fact that when Plant X workers were of high-school age a far higher proportion of eligibles attended high schools in the United States than in previous years.

There is a more specific reason for these proportions, however. Members of the company's employment staff stated that preference was generally given to men with high-school education. Since over 20,000 applications originally had been filed, and since there were only 1,400 to 1,700 potential job openings, it was not too difficult to find persons of high-school level for filling these positions.

Such facts pose an obvious question: Why was such emphasis placed on education when the nature of most assembly line jobs is such as to require little formal education? How important is education as a factor in determining a man's adjustment to assembly line work? At which educational levels will we find the greatest amount of satisfaction or dissatisfaction? The evidence in the present study is not conclusive, but the qualitative comments of some workers indicated that job satisfaction was inversely related to educational level.

INDEX

Absenteeism, 144; causes, 116–120; grievances and, 127
Absenteeism: Management's Problem, 118n
Advancement, aspirations, 107–114. *See also* Promotion and transfer
Age, average, 36; differences, 67n; effect on attitude toward company, 135; company policy on, 172
Agriculture, small recruitment, 32
American Society of Mechanical Engineers, Management Division, 153n
Anonymity of worker, 160–161
Antagonisms, 67n
Applications for jobs, 82
Assembly line jobs, attitudes toward, 39, 44–45; and advancement aspirations, 113–114
Assistant superintendent, 92
Attention to work, requirements, 69
Attitudes of workers, to jobs, 50–65, 115, 142–144; to union, 123, 128–133; to company, 135–140; handling in questionnaires, 169–171
Automobile assembly line, need for study, 4–5; characteristics, 13–14, 19–20; description, 22–27
Automobile industry, wages, 82, 84–85; union policy, 85; labor turnover, 116–117

Baffle windbreaker assembler, 44–45
"Bank building," 146–147
Behavior, and mass production characteristics, 115–122, 141, 144
Below Median Job Factor Score, 119, 120
Bias, questionnaire elimination, 168
Blower-defroster assembler, 47
Body assembly, 21, 22–25
"Body drop," 25, 26
Body in White (metal) Department, 22. *See also* Metal Department
Bonderizing (anti-rust) paint, 24
Bonus system, absence of, 86
Bristol-Myer Company, 150n
British Industrial Fatigue Research Board, 14n, 116n
Bureau of Labor Statistics (U.S. Department of Labor), 116, 116n

Capitalism, worker attitudes, 144
Car conditioning line, 26
Car conditioning, repairman, 47–49
Car Distribution Department, 22
Chassis assembly, 21, 25–26
Chassis Department, 22; repairman, 47–49; utilityman, 49–50; social interaction, 69–70
Choice of tools and techniques, absence of, 36–37. *See also* Predetermination of tools and techniques

Clague, Ewan, 2n
Collective bargaining, 85
Community, coöperation, 165
Company, worker attitudes, 135–140
Company policy, 94, 107–108
Comparative rating on job characteristics, 43, 61–64
Comptroller's office, 22
Congress of Industrial Organizations, 123, 134, 159n
Conveyor system, automobile industry, 13; description, 22, 24–25, 27; determinant of pace, 85–86; worker dislike, 145–146
Coöperation in interviews, 164–167
Craft skills, elimination, 85

Depersonalization, 160–161
Dictionary of Occupational Titles, 30, 41
Dingman (repairman), 42
Disciplinary action, union attitude, 124–125; grievances, 127
Discrimination, absence of, 133
Dislike factors, rating, 62; job content, 63–65; social aspects of job, 68; economic aspects, 90; working conditions, 105; advancement prospects, 112–113; union, 132
Distribution of jobs analyzed, 51
Drucker, Peter, suggestions on predetermination of tools and techniques, 153–154; *The Human Being in Industrial Production*, 153n
Dwelling status, workers', 173–174

Economic factors, 81, 142; and job content, 64; data, 81–86; worker comments, 87–89, 142; relation to other job elements, 89–91; advancement aspirations, 111
Education of workers, 36, 174; effect on attitudes toward company, 135–136; company policies, 174–175
Emotional criticism, 138–140
Encyclopedia Britannica, 10n
English factories, 116
Europe, development of industrialization, 162–163
Experimentation, 151, 153

Factual data, in interviews, 169
Fatigue, and previous jobs, 37n
Financial incentive, 108
Ford, Henry, quoted, 10, 10n, 13
Ford, Henry, II, quoted, 1
Foreman, functions, 92; worker relations, 92–100, 143; promotions to, 107n; aspirations to become, 109–111, 144; interaction with workers, 157–158
Fox, J. B., absenteeism study, 118n
Fractionalizing, social effects, 159